Palgrave Pivots in Sports Economics

Series Editors
Wladimir Andreff, Emeritus Professor, University Paris 1
Panthéon-Sorbonne, Paris, France
Andrew Zimbalist, Department of Economics, Smith College,
Northampton, MA, USA

This mid-length monograph series invites contributions between 25,000–50,000 words in length, and considers the economic analysis of sports from all aspects, including but not limited to: the demand for sports, broadcasting and media, sport and health, mega-events, sports accounting, finance, betting and gambling, sponsorship, regional development, governance, competitive balance, revenue sharing, player unions, pricing and ticketing, regulation and anti-trust, and, globalization. Sports Economics is a rapidly growing field and this series provides an exciting new publication outlet enabling authors to generate reach and impact.

More information about this series at
http://www.palgrave.com/gp/series/15189

Jorge Tovar

On Fairness, Justice, and VAR

Russia 2018 and France 2019 World Cups
in a Historical Perspective

Jorge Tovar
Department of Economics
Universidad de Los Andes
Bogota, Colombia

ISSN 2662-6438   ISSN 2662-6446   (electronic)
Palgrave Pivots in Sports Economics
ISBN 978-3-030-84813-2   ISBN 978-3-030-84814-9   (eBook)
https://doi.org/10.1007/978-3-030-84814-9

This Palgrave Macmillan imprint is published by the registered company Springer Nature Switzerland AG
The registered company address is: Gewerbestrasse 11, 6330 Cham, Switzerland

Andrea Catalina
Gracias a esas charlas contigo, impregnadas de entusiasmo juvenil, he
podido finalizar este proyecto en medio de la pandemia y de tantas
dificultades personales. Te agradezco las lecciones sobre constancia,
concentración y esfuerzo como requisitos necesarios para alcanzar los
objetivos.
Esa llamada diaria, un halo de esperanza e ilusión.
El papá, con mucho amor.

Contents

LIST OF FIGURES

CHAPTER 1

Introduction

Abstract The video assistant referee (VAR) is the most important technological breakthrough in the history of soccer. Since its inception, the sport has shaped its institutions to adapt to the ever-changing conditions. This chapter motivates the book showing how the quest for justice has been a continuous process since the foundation of the modern game in 1863.

Keywords FIFA World Cup Russia 2018 · FIFA World Cup France 2019 · Video Assistant Referee · Theory of Justice · Fairness · Soccer

No, it will not erase it. It is not about taking revenge on our behalf. It would be perfect if the French beat Germany, yes. But no "bleus" victory will classify us for the 1982 World Cup final.

Alain Giresse, a 1982 French player, asked if a French victory over Germany in Brazil 2014 would make their semifinal defeat against the Germans go into oblivion.[1]

---

[1] https://elpais.com/deportes/2014/07/03/mundial_futbol/1404416221_854085.html visited May 29, 2021.

© The Author(s), under exclusive license to Springer Nature Switzerland AG 2021
J. Tovar, *On Fairness, Justice, and VAR*,
Palgrave Pivots in Sports Economics,
https://doi.org/10.1007/978-3-030-84814-9_1

The video assistant referee (VAR) is arguably FIFA's, the historically conservative ruling body of world soccer, most important technological breakthrough and the most significant effort to enforce the rules of the game since its foundation in 1904. Although tested in some prior events, its grand debut occurred in the Russia 2018 FIFA World Cup. VAR is nothing else but the use of video technology to determine whether a referee's decision (or lack of it) is right or wrong. The simplicity of its purpose does not hide the enormous repercussion that it has over the sport, as some argue that it is the ultimate weapon to bring justice to soccer. In contrast, others state that VAR has the potential to destroy its essence.

Mexico 1970 was the last Word Cup that Pelé would play, for many of us, the best soccer player of all time. His performance in the semifinal against Uruguay was nothing short o f what the world was expecting. In four games, Pelé had already scored three goals and made three assists. Moreover, he had already performed two of the three magical movements recorded in history as the World Cup's best no-goals. Against Czechoslovakia, the shot from his own half, hitherto unseen in a World Cup, was just inches away from the surprised goalkeeper. Days later, facing England, Pelé headed a right cross from Jairzinho with surprising strength making the ball bounce a meter before crossing the goal line. It was a goal, and as such, the Jalisco Stadium began celebrations. Banks, England's goalkeeper, thought otherwise. His feline dive to the right denied the goal, sending the ball above the bar, making it the most amazing save in World Cup history.

On the way to the final, June 17, 1970, Brazil had to face its ghosts playing again in Guadalajara. Uruguay, the same nation that had sparked the largest disaster in Brazil's sporting history (and maybe even beyond), the 1950 *Maracanazo*, was the only obstacle remaining before the final. In a challenging game, with Uruguay down 2–1 in the second half, Pelé picked the ball in his own half and rushed parallel to the line in a dangerous counterattack. When leveled with the Uruguayan box, the ball went a bit long. Fontes, defending the Brazilian, accelerated to cut the attack before Pelé had the ball again under control. However, Pelé managed to block the defender by using his body to shield the ball. He slightly slowed the pace. When Fontes was near enough, Pelé raised his right arm and elbowed him in the face. The only available image I know of on YouTube is shocking.[2] Fontes's head bounces back and forth while he is attempting to tackle the Brazilian. True, Fontes' tackle intentions did not seem innocent. The referee called a free kick for Brazil, ignoring (or maybe not seeing) Pelé's elbow aggression. Later that game, Pelé assisted Rivelino for Brazil's third goal and even had time to execute the third magical no-goal movement when he dribbled the Uruguayan goalkeeper Mazurkiewicz without touching the ball.

Brazil won 3–1, and Pelé played the final, entering forever into soccer's history as "The King." Had the VAR existed, Pelé might have been barred from the final. Nevertheless, even if he had been sent off, Pelé might have played the final as did Garrincha in 1962 after being sent off in the semi-final against Chile. However, absent from the final, the remembrances of his performance in that game would be all but a counterfactual. Without Pelé, Brazil was still a top team, but it is worth noting that against Italy, The King scored once and assisted twice. Maybe, in 1970, Brazil, arguably the best team in history, would not have won the World Cup.

Despite not sending Pelé off, the Brazilian press titled "Not even the referees can stop Brazil."[3] The story so far suggests that the referee's ruling was detrimental for the Uruguayans. However, at least two chances could have been a penalty kick for Brazil, and the Uruguayans' defensive aggressiveness was the predominant characteristic of their game. Although slightly fanatic, maybe the headline is understandable.

Was it fair for Pelé to be allowed to play the final? Was justice made (or not) when the referee chose not to send off the Brazilian star? Was Brazil's victory a fair result? These are questions with unclear answers; it might even be pretentious to claim the existence of a correct answer. Nevertheless, they are valid questions worth exploring to contribute to the ongoing debate of the usefulness of implementing the VAR in soccer.

Implicit and explicitly, the continuous quest for justice supports the implementation of the VAR technology. The rules of the game dictate that the referee is the person who decides whether a given circumstance is legal or not. But justice is a fluid concept with a long-standing debate in various disciplines. Referees are humans, as are players, managers, fans, and reporters. Thus, by definition, the game is prone to involuntary

---

[2] https://youtu.be/CfMrusSAWJU?t=825, visited January 10th, 2021.

[3] ABC newspaper June 19, 1970, p. 46.

mistakes. The referee may find herself far away; there might be an obstruction in her line of sight, or simply, given the circumstances, she thought that the decision made was the appropriate one. In principle, technology can overcome such human limitations. The objective of implementing VAR was never to reduce mistakes to zero. However, currently, VAR seeks to minimize such errors. Make it a fairer game.

This book draws from the long-lasting debate on the theory of justice to analyze the role of justice and fairness in soccer. Not surprisingly, no philosopher, to the best of my knowledge, over two millennia has explicitly thought about the problem of justice in the context of a sporting industry. The general focus, primarily on distributive justice, is exploring and theorizing, within a society, how to allocate scarce resources among agents whose needs and claims overlap. Economists and political philosophers have coincided in the debate for a long time, albeit with methodological differences. Economists find the philosophers' way of thinking too informal. In contrast, philosophers are interested in the "intellectual process that precedes the formulation of the model" (Roemer, 1998, p. 2) instead of the inference procedure executed by economists.

The book's objective is to use the existing literature to understand the quest for justice in soccer. There is no intention of being part of the debate or extensively reviewing the literature on justice theories. The novelty of the approach is the use of some key concepts about the ideas of justice while drawing a path through which one can understand the persistent quest for justice and fairness in soccer without forgetting that these theories seek to explain broader aspects of societies. They theorize on how to design a just and/or fair society. In many facets, much of the concepts to improve society are empirically tricky, if not impossible to implement. However, particularly when reviewing economists' work, plenty of experiments and numerical examples give a quantitative approach to the theory. In other words, while most theories of justice seek the ideal institutions to build just societies, their use "for global as well as national judgements mainly lie in being able to compare social alternatives, none of which have the superlative quality of being ideal or perfect" (Sen, 2017, p. 265). For example, Sen (2017) argues that the objective of a slaveless society was not perfection but a less unjust one.

Moreover, alternative questions on justice do not necessarily imply complete agreements. Whether Pelé was expelled or not may have been unfair for Uruguayans, but not for Brazilians. Or, abstracting from a nationalistic point of view, it might not have been just for those who love the artistic abilities of the Brazilian relative to Fontes's less fanciful style.

Soccer has evolved hand in hand with society. The genesis of modern soccer was in English public schools where the elite's sons went to study. A homogenous social class eased the design of standardized rules enforced by a set of common codes. Although the concept of the referee was discussed while drafting the original 1863 rules (Wernicke, 2017), the gentlemen's character of the game deemed an enforcer unnecessary. As time passed, the latter was no longer valid because, as soccer expanded across classes, the game evolved. To some, it was an undesirable trait. In 1890, Pierre de Coubertin, the founder of the modern Olympic Games, held that "played by miners and workers in large factories, people who do not stand out precisely for their gentlemen spirit, soccer necessarily becomes brute and risky, while played by well-educated young people it remains as what it is, an excellent exercise of dexterity, agility, strength and cold blood to which it is possible to surrender without renouncing the rules of courtesy."[4]

By the time of the first FA Cup final, 1872, the teams agreed that each one would have an official who from the sideline would guarantee that the rules were adequately applied (Wernicke, 2017). They were there to ensure a just and fair game, but still, the rules had no mention of officials or umpires until 1874 (Goldblatt, 2007). Since then, the soccer rules, supervised by the International Football Association Board (IFAB), founded in 1886, have continuously evolved to adapt themselves to the game's needs.

The pursuit of justice moves hand in hand with the idea of fairness. The concept of justice, as soccer itself, is an evolutionary phenomenon where judgments are not universally independent of time, making fairness a dynamic notion, one that has evolved following the conventions that emerge from contemporary cultural influences. As societies interact, individuals realized that social arrangements are human-created rather than natural phenomena (Barry, 1989). It was under the umbrella of the need for justice in a social context that FIFA implemented such a significant technological change. Thus, to understand such concepts within the soccer environment, I draw from the justice literature to contextualize the

[4] Cited in Correia (2019, p. 88).

historical importance of the VAR implementation within the society that soccer is in itself.

When exploring the background of justice, fairness, and the VAR implementation, it is helpful to review the utilization of the new technology in the topmost soccer events: the men's 2018 and women's 2019 FIFA World Cup. Using event-level data for each game of the World Cup, the book describes each tournament's evolution, focusing on the practical operations of the VAR. It goes beyond the number of times used by doing an analytical description of the VAR-related events.

The book ultimately connects the concepts of justice and fairness with the implementation of VAR. Using the VAR-related events that happened during Russia 2018 and France 2019, one can historically review controversial actions that help understand the impact of modern technology on soccer. The objective is not to rewrite history, an impossible and useless task. The counterfactual exercises connect to the debate on what is fair and how just was the decisions taken during the men's and women's World Cups, prompting action to better implement the technology in the most influential sport of our time. The debate might seem out of focus to those who believe that little can be learned from reviewing the debate from a philosophical perspective after implementing such structural changes. In that sense, I would direct them to Barry (1989), who in the introduction of the third section of his book starts to study questions on the method in moral philosophy, which he discussed in the first half: "normally the practice comes first and the philosophy attempts to make sense of it after the fact" (p. 258). This book is not a philosophy treaty, nor does it try to be, but it uses some of its concepts to advance in understanding justice in soccer.

The book reviews a diversity of theories of justice to understand the evolution of the sport and the logic behind the recent structural changes in implementing the existing rules. Justice is the process of designing the guidelines that build society. When dealing with distributive justice, a common feature in the literature, the design behind the theory is t o create a system that derives in a society that complies with the necessary standards of a just society given some dimension. Building an optimal and just system is a process that in soccer proxies to the evolution of its guidelines, i.e., the rules of the game. Hence, reviewing the process's beginning and dynamics leads to understanding the implementation of new mechanisms, even as disruptive as the VAR technology.

Considering soccer, a society on its own, justice relates to the existence of a well-known and universally accepted set of rules which need to be appropriately applied to achieve fairness. The arbitrator, in soccer, the referee, needs to have complete knowledge of the rules and master the capacity to implement them under conditions that are, in some situations, far more complex than what judges do in other areas of society. The pressure of a billion people judging one's decision can be overwhelming.

Thus, referees are just when correctly applying the rules of the game. They might be fair or unfair because a consensus is scarcer than one would desire when interpreting the law. Currently, no machine can generate complete agreement on all decisions in the sport. VAR seeks to minimize disagreements. It is not clear that it is achieving its goals. Injustice arrives when referees do not use the tools at their disposal. We will see that it is more common than one could think a priori.

After reviewing how VAR impacted Russia 2018 and France 2019 and examining relevant events of the World Cup history, the conclusion is that injustice is unavoidable, and complete fairness is unachievable. It remains to discuss the role of the VAR and how to extract the best of the mechanism.

The book is comprised of six chapters, including this introduction. Chapter 2 reviews various theories of justice to set the grounds of what we understand for justice and fairness in the context of soccer and the history of the World Cups. Chapter 3 describes the path followed until the IFAB approved the use of the VAR technology. It also reviews the existing literature on VAR and its impact on soccer. Chapter 4 explores quantitatively and qualitatively the use of VAR in both Russia 2018 and France 2019. Using event-level data, it draws on Chapter 2 conceptions to understand justice and fairness, complementing findings, when necessary, with a historical approach. Chapter 5 gathers all the available information to discuss the role of VAR in terms of justice and fairness. It develops a proposal on how to advance with the VAR mechanism. Last, Chapter 6 presents the conclusions.

References

Barry, B. (1989). *Theories of justice*. University of California Press.

Correia, M. (2019). *Una historia popular del fútbol*. Hoja de Lata editorial. Xixón, Asturies (España).

Goldblatt, D. (2007). *The ball is round: A global history of football*. Penguin.

Roemer, J. E. (1998). *Theories of distributive justice*. Harvard University Press.

Sen, A. (2017). Ethics and the foundation of global justice. *Ethics & International Affairs, 31*(3), 261–270.

Wernicke, L. (2017). *¿Por qué juegan once contra once?* Planeta Colombia.

CHAPTER 2

Justice and Fairness

Abstract This chapter draws from the theory of justice to explore the role of justice and fairness in soccer. Reviewing the writings of a variety of prominent thinkers, it seeks to understand the evolution of soccer's institutions and the role of an arbitrator within a maximizing welfare objective. It uses controversial historical situations in the history of the World Cup to contextualize the philosophical debate with the world of soccer. The novelty of the approach is to build a theoretical framework that allows the reader to comprehend the complexity of achieving consensus, not only in society but also in soccer.

Keywords Justice · Fairness · Society well-being · Social contract · Original Position · Equality

I am indebted to Andrés Alvarez and Jimena Hurtado, colleagues at the University of Los Andes and professors of the history of economic thought, for reading and sharing their comments on an earlier version of this chapter. The final edition is mine and does not compromise them. Considering the novelty of the chapter, blending two distinct areas of research, in principle so far apart, I am extremely grateful for their suggestions on what additional literature to review and on how to improve the flow of my ideas.

J. Tovar, *On Fairness, Justice, and VAR*, Palgrave Pivots in Sports Economics, https://doi.org/10.1007/978-3-030-84814-9_2

9

There is a long tradition of exploring the meaning of justice and fairness among philosophers, economists, and other social scientists. The vastness of the debate makes it very difficult to cite a unique definition of justice because, in many ways, it depends on the historical, political, and social context in which each author studied the concept.

Overall, justice is a relative concept which involves reasoning, perception, and a sense of injustice to compare it with. The quest for justice and its meaning "is one that arises in any society whenever its members start to think reflectively about the arrangements within which their lives are lived" and theories on it thrive on theorizing "about the kinds of social arrangements that can be defined" (Barry, 1989, p. 3). Following this statement, individuals can claim justice when analyzing their place in society while seeking impartial enforcement of some given rules. Relevant for the exercise at hand, there must be an agent, given the claims and the existing regulations, willing to impartially distribute justice.

Among the early thinkers, Plato was arguably the first to study the meaning of justice. Over two thousand years later, there is no one unique form of justice. One could review the concept from the point of view of distributive justice, justice as a virtue, or retributive justice, among many alternatives. The complexities of such debate are well beyond the scope of this book, thus the need to narrow it. This chapter is centered on how the rules came to be; therefore, it borrows heavily from the discussions on contractualism, the idea where a socially accepted contract supports morality.

Additionally, interest focuses on who enforces the rules, not just in the institutional design that approves the rules. Indeed, in the small society that soccer is, the prevalent social framework results in a distribution of benefits and burdens across agents, much like in any "global" society. Distributive justice emerges from disseminating income, wealth, or other similar indicators among members of the society, be they individuals, groups, or other groupings seeking equality, some type of maximization, or another distributional objective. In the case of soccer, the arbitrator makes, ideally, impartial decisions based on some given rules. Overlapping various concepts and streams of thought is not a novelty, but it must be tactfully done to clearly guarantee that the ideas flow. The effort in this chapter seeks to understand how rules came to be, how they are enforced, and who benefits or not from them, using as a theoretical background various approaches to a theory of justice.

If Plato was the pioneer, Aristotle set the pace when stating distributive justice theory as a proportionality concept, where equals should be treated as equals and unequal's unequally (Moulin, 2004), implying that distributive justice is concerned with fair outcomes. Soccer-wise, the rules of the game, which the referee is to enforce, relate, for instance, to fairness when a penalty kick is "correctly" called. However, as any soccer fan knows, sometimes the referee calls a foul when the entire stadium saw otherwise, or vice versa. Either way, soccer has a "social contract," which, if defined as in Locke, Rousseau, or Kant, can be thought of as a hypothetical order alternative to "the chaos that might otherwise characterize a society" (Sen, 2009, p. 6). Following these precepts, Rawls, the most influential contract theorist of, at least, the past century, framed his principles of justice on an original agreement that defined society's basic structure. This agreement stems from an original position, nothing else than a hypothetical situation in which people are unaware of their place in society, making them equals within a veil of ignorance. Given people's rationality, this veil of ignorance lays the framework for a unanimous conception of justice (Konow, 2003).

Putting aside the validity of Rawls' hypothetical original position (and the fact that the principles of justice are ideal distributional mechanisms), soccer's initial social contract is key in understanding the expansion of the sport. In its modern version, established in 1863, soccer was a gentlemen's game where players, the captains, oversaw the rules; they called the fouls. Soccer's original position, in Rawls's sense, was this early period with justice based on the idea of equals, where the expectation was that everyone on the pitch would behave like a gentleman. Although not literally, the conception of justice among those who designed the early soccer institutions was unanimous. Still, unlike in Rawls's argument, individuals were aware of their position within the soccer community, but they had a sense of equality hard to find in other areas of society.

A contract, as described above, seeks to offer a mechanism through which to distribute justice fairly. The arrival of impartial referees in the late nineteenth century symbolizes the dawn of a new era where players are no longer neutral "gentlemen," and there is a need for an external authority to enforce justice. The existence of an impartial judge combined with clear rules of the game should be enough to guarantee a fair and just game. Indeed, the simplicity of the game and its rules partially explains why soccer expanded so fast across the world during the last decade of the nineteenth century and the first quarter of the twentieth century.

However, as the sport expanded, the rules and the referee were not enough to guarantee a just game. The existing social contract was insufficient to distribute justice fairly. Controversy and a sense of injustice started as soon as Uruguay 1930, during the first World Cup. During the semifinal between Yugoslavia and hosts Uruguay, the former questionably got chalked off a goal when losing 2–1. With no VAR to check, history says that minutes later, when the ball went out of play, a policeman near the sideline kicked the ball back, leading to Uruguay's third goal. The game would end up with Uruguay winning 6–1. Earlier on the tournament, that same referee, the Brazilian Gilberto Rego, had already made a major controversial decision. Having the Argentinian Monti scored the only goal in the game against France during the group phase, Rego finished the game three minutes early. Reverend Dr. Martin Luther King Jr. noted, "injustice anywhere is a threat to justice everywhere" (cited in Sen, 2017, p. 261).

Rawls's theory of justice requires the "need for objectivity through impartiality, in a way that one's own interests do not bias what one argues for" Sen (2017, p. 264). Little is known about Rego's biases; maybe he was just a lousy referee, but he lived in an era well past the gentlemen's ideals of equality within the game. Perhaps because he was aware of his self-preferences, he was unable to decide behind a veil of ignorance, making his decisions unfair towards the European teams that traveled for weeks across the Atlantic. It is the demand for fairness that drives the need to avoid biases in how individuals evaluate and decide. It leads to the pursuit of justice. Based on the original position, Rawls's demands of impartiality lead to unanimously chosen principles of justice. These, in turn, determine the social institutions that should govern society. In Rawls's setup, fairness and justice will rise from the unanimously chosen principles of justice derived from the veil of ignorance. Indeed, fairness is fundamental to justice.

The idealization of the early days in soccer is stretching a bit far from Rawls's writings on the original position. The gentlemen's game was an activity that evolved as it required. Not only did soccer move from its upper-class strongholds to middle- and working-class neighborhoods, but even among the former, the game changed because even soccer's *original position* was not impartial enough in Rawls's sense. Impartiality was incomplete, and the rules proved insufficient to satisfy the contract's objective of distributing justice fairly. The rigid crossbar above the two goalposts, established in 1882, derived from a tape strung between the posts in the late 1870s when a goal was allowed despite the ball passing (between the posts) about thirty meters up in the air (Goldblatt, 2007).

Yes, it is stretching it a bit, but the sense that this sport in the early days was a different game, a game where gentlemen had a particular morality set, is engraved in the world of soccer. As early as 1930, when recalling the "old times," *Mundo Uruguayo* writes:

> Lads, in the old days, didn't use hair gel. (…) Well: the point is that on this page, we try to evoke a time that is long gone, that is very distant in the memory of our people, but that has undoubtedly been the most important in the life of Uruguayan *foot-ball*. At that time, there were no large stadiums; it was played in concealed pastures which were pompously given the title of fields. The *players* were not stars for any fan; they were those crazy Englishmen who spent hours kicking a leather ball. At that time, the players did not receive large salaries: instead, they had to pay rent to use the field in which they practiced. And it was that *foot-ball*, perhaps less polished than the one played nowadays, perhaps less elegant, but much more enthusiastic; back then, they defended the colors of a T-shirt, not the colors of a banknote.[1]

Although it makes sense to try to understand the need and requirements for justice from the writings of political philosophers, one must keep in mind that Rawls's statements stem from hypothetical scenarios that eventually lead to normative states of society. Rawls or any other thinker seeks to find a path to a better society defined in some way, well-being, for instance. Thus, their arguments are but a methodological course to better understand how justice in soccer evolved.

The first stage of Rawls's theory of justice consists of the two principles of justice. The first one deals with equal rights and a complete scheme of liberties for all. The second, comprised of two parts, understands that social and economic inequalities need to satisfy fair equality of opportunity and that the least advantaged members of society must benefit the most. Translating it to the soccer environment, it seems that the first principle is unambiguously fulfilled. Unless illegal maneuvers are at play, both teams face the same rights and duties in any soccer match. A similar argument can be made regarding the first part of the second principle of justice. All players in a game have access, by and large, to

---

[1] Mundo Uruguayo, July 31, 1930, Año XII, Núm. 603, p. 45. Own translation. Words in italics are originally in English.

the same level of justice. Assuming Rego's best intentions and innocent of any wrongdoing, every team he refereed had equal opportunities to access a fair and just system.

The second part of Rawls's second principle of justice can be left out when dealing with sports because of the intrinsic difficulty of defining the least advantaged members of this specific *society*. More importantly, Rawls's arguments deal with income and well-being. It makes sense in that context that individuals require not only equal opportunities but that they also benefit more when in distress. In sports, talent is a given, a definitively not uniformly distributed characteristic that leads to inequalities. In Rawls's distributive theory, productivities are a source of inequalities, and they are valid as long as they take the worst off to be better off. Despite the latter, in soccer, with the structure of the game in mind, it is difficult to explain why aid teams or players who are at a sporting disadvantage. One could immerse into a discussion of competitive balance, where teams in a league should not differ qualitatively excessively between each other. This, however, pushes the argument beyond the objectives of the discussion. The interest is to understand how the game is played, literally each game, and how VAR came to be following the eternal search for justice.

It follows from the above that soccer, if seen isolated from the rest of society, arguably follows the precepts and concepts that makes it a just and fair environment to prosper. The design of a unique set of rules in 1863 and the establishment of a solid institution to enforce such *just* and *unanimously chosen* rules, the Football Association in England, seeds the conception of justice imagined (broadly speaking) by Rawls.

But just as Rawls's views have been heavily disputed over the years, it is not farfetched to state that the social contract, even if it at some point was idyllic in the Rawlsian sense, needs to evolve. It is in human nature to change, and the gentlemen's game was promptly abandoned, not only as the game expanded across classes but also across countries, continents, and, consequently, cultures. The idea that individuals will spontaneously move as projected in the original position has limits in human behavior, even more in a game that moved towards a professionalization phase where winning was more than just a sporting result.

The World Cup of Italy 1934 is the ultimate example of the growing importance of soccer, far beyond its own little round world. "Italy must win," exclaimed Mussolini, the Italian fascist Prime Minister at the time. Giorgio Vaccaro, the President of the Italian Soccer Federation, diplomatically responded that they "would do their best." Mussolini made himself clear: "You do not understand. It is an order. Italy must win the World Cup" (Tovar, 2014).

In the quarterfinals, Italy played a great Spanish team led by the magnificent goalkeeper Ricardo Zamora, known as "El Divino," literally the Divine, for his out-of-earth abilities to stop the ball from crossing the goal line. At the time, if a game ended in a draw, a rematch should be played the day after. Spain had the lead until Schiavio grabbed Zamora, which allowed Ferrari to equalize the game that ended 1–1. More importantly, seven Spanish players, including Zamora with two broken ribs, were unable to play the second match. Italy also suffered from the battle: four of its players were out. Italy won the rematch 1–0. The Swiss referee, Mercet, who invalidated two Spanish goals, would never again referee an international match and was eventually expelled by FIFA and the Swiss Federation. Italy would go on to win their first world championship.

Justice comes in many flavors, but it stems from inequalities, as Plato remarked a couple of millennia ago when he noted that law arose when the cost of injustice was greater to people than the benefits of having it (Barry, 1989). Justice, thus, surfaces from those in advantage who recognize that society will improve and become stronger if people cooperate with each other as opposed to continuous conflict. Even in a Rawlsian sense, the rules of soccer originate in the pursuit of equality, i.e., the need to avoid unfairness in a game expected to glorify the best by merit. From this point of view, justice "is the name we give to the constraints on themselves that rational self-interested people would agree to as the minimum price that has to be paid in order to obtain the cooperation of others" (Barry, 1989, p. 7).

Rawls's concept, where individuals would spontaneously do what they had agreed in their original position, is empirically challenging to sustain, even in the early stages of the gentlemen's game when many hypothetical precepts can be related to the historical facts. The idea that just institutions born under the conditions already discussed in a Rawlsian world are enough seems to undermine the human component. For practical use, a theory of justice cannot ignore behavioral patterns such as greed, corruption, or cupidity (Sen, 2017). When dealing with soccer, its institutions exert a monopoly power on the sport's operations worldwide. Despite temporary historical deviations in certain countries, each one has a unique Football Association, following the English one established in 1863. FIFA, founded in 1904, rules world soccer with more members than the United Nations (Tovar, 2021). FIFA then joined IFAB contributing to control the rules of the game in a centralized manner. Overall, the institutional structure is set such that justice spreads across soccer pitches around the world. However, it is in human nature to cheat, deceive, and exploit potential advantages. Thus, these soccer institutions are but agents recognizing that public discussion can alter people's responsibilities and influence their behavior, an essential element when pursuing justice.

The sense of justice (or injustice) changes with time. Consider the 1954 World Cup Final played in Bern between Germany and Hungary. There is more than one side to the story of what happened that day in Switzerland. Hungary, undefeated since 1950, current Olympic champions, had reached the final after defeating South American giants Brazil in the quarterfinals and Uruguay in the semifinals. The former erupted in aggression and bottles flying both ways, while the latter was the first defeat of the Uruguayans in the World Cup history. Uruguay only lost in extra time while having players injured outside the field. Germany had relatively simple games against Yugoslavia in the quarterfinals and Austria in the semifinal on the other side of the draw.

The game day was ready. It rained the day before. It rained heavily during the second part, making it a muddy pitch that hampered the Hungarian passing game. This is important for what happened during the game. Puskas, the Hungarian star, had been injured in the group phase game against Germany. He forced himself to play the final. His effort seemed to pay when his team had a two-goal lead by the eighth minute, having himself scored once. Germany, however, came back. Ten minutes later, the game was 2–2. Just six minutes before the final whistle, Rahn scored the third goal for Germany.

The game was not yet over. The Hungarian machine still had time to score an additional goal. The referee called an offside. The only video available, to the best of my knowledge, is inconclusive. It runs too late in the play, and when the pass came, it is not possible to determine with certainty Puskas' position.[2] However, it does raise some doubts. When Puskas receives the ball and enters the area tilted towards the left flank, at least two defenders, closer to the goalkeeper than him, are running diagonally from the right side. On that play, Puskas said that

---

[2] https://www.youtube.com/watch?v=ulxTJT1OZdM, visited March 3, 2021.

the "Welsh linesman who had refereed the game against Uruguay, disallowed it for offside, despite the fact that the English referee, Bill Ling, had concede it. When he raised the flag, we were already in the center circle" (Taylor & Jamrich, 2018). Puskas always maintained that the flag went up almost a minute after he had scored. In an interview hours after the game, he claimed that "the goal disallowed was indisputably legitimate."[3] Even "the English referee Billy Ling had given it" he declared (Goldblatt, 2007, p. 352). Moreover, Sebes, the Hungarian coach, complained about the referee's nationality: "isn't it odd we always seem to get British referees?" (Goldblatt, 2007, p. 352). On the other side, the goal simply was "controversially disallowed" (Hesse, 2003).

The legend around the "Miracle of Bern" is unparallel. Beyond some not fully proven accusations of doping with pervitin, methamphetamine used by German soldiers during World War 2, there is also the story of the Adidas boots.[4] The company supplied boots with removable studs, a significant technological advance at the time. As had occurred during the entire tournament, the weather was rainy and the field muddy, which by itself was a negative factor for the fantastic Hungarian style. The boots' role will never be fully determined, but the technological advantage could have made a difference. The latter is a debate beyond the scope of this book, but whatever the effect, the unfairness (or not) of allowing such a technological gap is open to discussion. Years later, in 2004, FIFA banned a simpler innovation. Cameroon used an all-in-one uniform because, according to Joseph Blatter, then FIFA's President, it was against the rules of the game. The rules he said at the time required one shirt, one shorts, and one pair of socks. The disparity in decisions towards innovations simply states the evolving sense of rule-keeping in the game.

Could the Hungarian defeat be unfair because the team was unbeaten for four years, a potentially legal goal disallowed, the Germans used unseen removable studs, and the world admired its tactical innovations? (see Wilson, 2013 on the latter). The unfairness of the German victory seems a strong statement if one believes, as Kahneman et al. (1986), that fairness cannot be understood without considering a reference point.

---

[3] El Bien Público, July 8, 1954, p. 5. Own Translation.

[4] Reuters, for instance, cites sport historian Erik Eggers claiming this doping theory. https://www.reuters.com/article/idINIndia-52485620101027, visited March 30, 2021.

Indeed, the use of technologically advanced football boots cannot make the result unfair if "fairness implies that some legal opportunities for gain are not exploited" (Kahneman et al., 1986). There was no rule against the removable studs as, if one believes Blatter, happened with Cameroon's uniform decades later.

Binmore (2009), going back to Rawls, argues that the final outcome must be egalitarian in the absence of external enforcement and assuming that the original position is sustainable by self-policing. In his theory, fairness relates to the distribution patterns where the less fortunate receive more than those that are better off. The precise amount depends on each society's cultural traits and its evolution. On the "Miracle of Bern," the Germans were the underdog, but even if Puskas's goal was illegally disallowed, soccer is not an area where fairness can be allocated based on unequal distributions of talent. It is in human nature to seek justice but also to justify the events. Grosics, the goalkeeper, years later complained about Puskas's goal but also about the second German goal.[5] A cross from the left, he jumped for the ball, as did Schäfer. Both missed the ball while clashing, mostly Grosics onto the German. The Hungarian does not explain why he claims that this goal is illegal, but one may assume that he believes that Schäfer obstructed him from grabbing the ball before it fell to Rahn, who scored the equalizer.

Of course, the discussion within any theory of justice tends to focus on the proper allocation of any kind of resources. Hungary was entitled to a righteous referee making fair decisions, and, indeed, there is no hard evidence that the linesman did any wrongdoing. Germany had the same rights to benefit from the law. The referee saw an offside. Nozick's entitlement theory, at least in its basic sense, seems to adjust well to what happened in Bern and many other previous and subsequent soccer games. In the absence of a central planner directing the evolution of the game, the final result was simply the reward obtained by the talent of each team. Nozick's view, libertarian as it is, cares little about the equality of the outcome, as long as the given agent achieves her objective by just means. In the sense that each team is entitled to its achievements, Nozick would state that the results are fair because "the justice of a state of affairs is a matter of whether individuals are entitled to their holdings" (Allingham,

---

[5] https://www.youtube.com/watch?v=4-8w85MzJcA, visited April 1, 2021.

2014, p. 58). Hungary might have had, a priori, more talent and modern tactics, but Germany proved that its merits were worthwhile.

For Nozick, as long as the world is "wholly just," his entitlement theory prevails (Allingham, 2014, p. 59). However, the problem in soccer (and probably in many other areas) is that societies are imperfect, and injustice exists. Theft, fraud, and other similar actions are unjust in that they block the voluntary transfer of justice. In the case of Puskas's third ghost goal, it matters little if the British referee's decision was morally correct or whether he acted on some impulsive belief (unconscious anti-communism, for instance). What matters is that for some observers, the offside ruling was unjust, maybe even fraudulent, propelling the feeling within the community that soccer requires continuous adjustment. It may be that although potentially both teams had access to the same distribution of justice, they may not have received a fair distribution of it.

Regardless of the referee's motives against the goal, the decision stands, and history cannot be rewritten. Maybe, if events such as those that occurred in 1954 Bern were isolated in time and space, the soccer community would not attempt to innovate in search of justice and fairness in the sport. However, the World Cup history is full of events where the end result may not have been fair, where justice could have been absent. The most famous and controversial decision in the World Cup history took place in the 1966 World Cup final between England and Germany. Again Germany, this time justice turned the back on them.

The founders of soccer, England, had reached the World Cup final for the first time. As the New York Times wrote in the chronicle of the final, "it was a match marked by the kind of hard clean play that had been noticeably absent from a number of the earlier games in the tournament."[6] With just one minute remaining, England fans at a packed Wembley Stadium were celebrating the 2–1 victory. At the very last minute, a free kick from Germany's left flank originated a confusing melee, culminating with Weber's dramatic goal. Banks, the legendary English goalkeeper, claimed a handball, more out of desperation than genuinely believing it. Extra time was unavoidable despite England's claim that Jackie Charlton had not fouled for a free kick.[7]

[6] *New York Times*, July 31, 1966, p. S6.
[7] *Sunday Mirror*, July 31, 1966, p. 15.

In the eleventh minute of extra time, Hurst, who had already scored the opening goal for England, received a ball just outside the six-yard box, his back to the goal, rotated to his left, and while falling shot with his right foot. The ball rose, passed buzzing next to Tilkowski's head, the German goalkeeper, and hit the underside of the crossbar. The strength of the shot made the ball bounce back to the field, just for Hunt to head and score. Unbelievable, the English forward chose not to attack the ball, turned around, lift his arms, and began to celebrate the goal. Meanwhile, Weber did what Hunt should have done. He went for the ball and cleared it far above the crossbar.

According to the New York Times' chronicle, the Soviet linesman, Tofiq Bahramov, initially indicated that the ball had not gone in.[8] The video of the game shows the referee, Gottfried Dienst, rushing towards the linesman just seconds after Weber's ball clearance. The talk ended in Dienst pointing towards the center of the field. The Germans surrounded Bahramov, but the official decision was immovable.

The shot, according to Reid and Zisserman (1996), who use "accurate metrology from uncalibrated video sequences," was at least 6 centimeters short of being a goal. The evidence at the time of the match, however, was naturally inconclusive. Minutes later, Germany was impacted again by another decision. In a last-minute counterattack, England, Hurst again, scored a fourth goal that should have been ruled out. A number of English fans, eager to celebrate, ran onto the pitch before the referee ended the game. While Hurst was running towards Tilkowski, the English commentator Wolstenholme chanted, "some people are on the pitch. They think it's all over." As Hurst scored, Wolstenholme continued, "It is now" (Waine & Naglo, 2013, p. 69).

The 1966 final, like the one in 1954, and Pele's elbow in the 1970 semifinal are all examples of how justice can potentially fail to achieve its objective: distributing justice fairly across all participants in every game of the World Cup. Following human nature, justice is a subjective concept when stakes are high, despite the existence of unambiguously accepted guidelines. While some see an offside, a ball passing the line, or an elbow out of place, others see the opposite. Consequently, fairness about the decisions taken is interpreted differently despite defined similarly: fairness is applying justice in an objective way.

---

[8] *New York Times*, July 31, 1966, p. S6.

The circle is accordingly complete. A universally just game seems impossible to reach. Suppose justice is subjective and fairness requires an objective application of justice. In that case, it seems implausible to have an event where all participants will permanently and unambiguously concur about their decisions.

Fairness, moreover, is not only about applying justice but also about its distribution. In soccer, the distribution of justice is even more complex because both parties can state that the other failed to comply with the rules of the game. Consider the English complaints where Jackie Charlton's challenge was not worthy of a foul, thus Weber's last-minute goal was undeserved, or Pele's elbow simply anticipating the strong Uruguayan tackle aiming at the King's ankle. The solution to the problem was defined as soon as the gentlemen's game stopped being so, as soon as soccer's "original position" became obsolete: the referee.

How can one determine if referees behave right or wrong? Scanlon states that an "act is wrong if its performance under the circumstances would be disallowed by any system of rules for the general regulation of behaviour which no one could reasonably reject as a basis for informed, unforced general agreement" (Scanlon, 1982, p. 110). He excludes agreements based o n false beliefs when expressing "informed agreement"; thus, a set of rules must exist. Unlike Rawls, who proposes a principle that everyone must agree to, Scanlon designs a principle which no one could reasonably reject. The former, however, is devising a general social framework, thus the need for the veil of ignorance. On the other hand, Scanlon is determining moral principles; the interest is to justify one's acts to the rest of society. Mercet, the 1934 Swiss referee, seems to have been unable to convince anyone about his decisions during Italy vs. Spain rematch. It looks like a case where he behaved unanimously wrong; his choices were unjust; thus, the Spanish team was treated unfairly. However, such unanimity is scarce in the history of the World Cup, and "wherever there is judgment, there is noise – and more than you think" (Kahneman et al., 2021).

In every modern soccer match, two teams face each other and, one might assume, are knowledgeable of a set of common rules. In any refereeless challenge between nearby neighborhoods playing in the local park for pride and little else, the rules are the same as those that govern World Cup games. Sometimes the rules are "simplified," and elements such as offsides are treated loosely. However, tackles and other specific actions are part of such a game's rules for the most part. Under soccer's "original position," the gentlemen, the captains, would bargain over how the rules should be applied. In the neighborhood challenge, it is not uncommon for the ball owner to simply leave if the rest of the players disagree with her interpretation of the rules. Alternatively, the game could end in an argument, which on occasions scales up to something more like a boxing event. At the top level, a game without a referee is nothing but a nonsense discussion. With fans, press, marketing, and the players themselves so involved in the game's outcome, it is nearly impossible to imagine a game without a referee figure.

The initial social contract, as understood above, allowed soccer to expand from its initial state in the nineteenth century. The entitlement theory, one might argue, fits well with the expansion of soccer across the world. At least when analyzing a trend, the allocation of talent reflects how the best players managed to generate excitement over the rest of the planet. Despite the numerous views of what happened in Bern in 1954, few, if any, question the German's legitimacy as World Champions. Not even the Hungarians.

However, at the match level, the teams' inability to systematically bargain and agree on how to dispense justice led to the continuous examination of the referees, those who must guarantee that the existing rules are appropriately applied.

Indeed, it all boils down to the figure of an arbitrator and how to guarantee that her actions follow the rules of the game, ensuring justice and fairness. Referees were nonexistent in the early rules, although such a figure varied according to the school. Some, like Cambridge or Eton, used a referee. Others like Brighton or Cheltenham let captains decide. In places like Charterhouse or Westminster, the contending parties made the decisions (Harvey, 2005).

Early referees, then called umpires, were first mentioned in 1874 and were drawn from each team. In the late 1870s, a third official would decide when the two umpires disagreed. This referee took charge of the game in 1891, but still, the captains called the fouls. Finally, in 1898, a neutral linesman replaced the umpires (Goldblatt, 2007).

A particular characteristic of soccer since the advent of cups, leagues, and other tournaments is the passion it generates among fans. People like to win, and when they cannot, it is not uncommon to discharge frustration and anger against others, in soccer, mostly referees.

Referees were abused since the dawn of time. In the post-war years, it is true in Germany; crowd trouble had the referee taken "to hospital under the protection of the military police" in Mülburgh (Hesse, 2003). Italy in the 1960s invented the *moviola*, the slow-motion repetition of controversial refereeing decisions. Spain has been blaming referees for almost every defeat of their national team since they lost against Italy in the 1924 Olympics (De Soto, 2015). Referees have even been killed, as happened in 1989 in Colombia. Referees are the main target of fans, players, but also of the sports governance structure.

The need for arbitration arises from the continuous conflicts of interest between the competing teams. In a non-sporting setting, justice could arise from the search for self-interest combined with differential bargaining powers leading to some kind of agreement. In soccer, bargaining power—defined as the ability to skew in any direction the rules of the game—is uniform across teams within a game unless, of course, one could show that powerful teams tend to benefit more from the referees' mistakes. However, even in such a case, in principle, the rules of the game are designed to dilute any differences in bargaining power.

In dealing with a just allocation of goods or services, the fair division is a concept defined as the equitable distribution of those that are "common property of a given set of microeconomic agents" (Moulin, 2004, p. 235). There is no distribution of commodities in soccer, but one can claim that each game has a set of just decisions to be made, and the expectations are for them to be fairly distributed over the match's length. Based on the latter, and assuming that there is no bargaining power to generate advantage for either team, justice may be defined as an agreement reached by rational people (Barry, 1989). This approach implies that justice arrives not from dealing with one's perspective but from seeking an acceptable agreement from all points of view.

Given the difficulty for agents to systematically agree, it seems natural to seek for a neutral third-party arbitrator to make the decisions, a common figure in theories of justice, when agents are self-interested, but also when they serve as an element to simulate the outcome of rational bargaining (Barry, 1989). The person making the decision should be impartial, easy said, difficult to define. In Rawls's sense, the impartial arbitrator would satisfy the requirement if she is unaware of her identity, making decisions under a veil of ignorance. Harsanyi's definition, less strict, defines the arbitrator as she who, while making the decisions, is aware of her identity and all the surrounding situation except that she has an equal probability of being either party in the dispute. Scanlon would seek no reasonable rejection from the decisions.

The arbitrator, the soccer referee, must behave impartially and follow some commonly agreed rules for the institution to have sustained credibility. This system of rules should be as universal as possible in dealing with potential events while facilitating an agreement between teams after a simple bargaining process. In Posner's words, "the law should as far as possible simulate the effects of perfect bargaining and allocate a right to the party that would have finished up with it as a result of bargaining" (Barry, 1989, p. 129). The fact that soccer games are possible in schoolyards, parks, and similar places implies that the game's rules abide, in some sense, by Posner's definition. In practice, however, the referee's capacity to fairly decide is limited by several factors, including the speed of the game, the player's willingness to mislead, and social pressure (Buraimo et al., 2010; Garicano et al., 2005). Even if these factors remained unseen, human beings tend to lack consensus when judging similar events. Exploring judges' decisions when facing comparable (if not equal) situations, Kahneman et al. (2021) find this to be the norm. Their analysis concludes that disagreement is unavoidable wherever judgment is involved.

Despite the lack of consensus about the decisions made, over time, the rules of the game have evolved to support the arbitrator in providing justice in the fairest way possible. The yellow and red cards, first available in a World Cup in 1970, were instruments to warn players in an attempt to scale down the violent actions observed in the 1966 World Cup.

Evolution started early in the game. An 1891 match between Stoke City and Aston Villa, for instance, led to the implementation of injury time. With the former losing 0–1, they were awarded a last-minute penalty kick. A Villa player kicked the (only) ball as far away as he could from the pitch showing little gallantry. Stoke players had no time to fetch and kick the penalty kick before time run out. An amendment to the rules was deemed necessary.

There have also been continuous technological adjustments to help referees. The 2004 IFAB minutes of the annual general meeting report that experiments using radio communication systems "between referees, assistants and the fourth official" had taken place in the Confederation Cup and the Scottish Premier League. At the time, IFAB was explicit about noting that such a system was not meant for broadcasting purposes.

There are, however, more often than less unintended effects. The bias in yellow cards favoring home teams is well known, a feature commonly explained by social pressure, as the absence of fans during the coronavirus pandemic suggests (Bryson et al., 2021). Garicano et al. (2005) provide evidence that referees systematically favor home teams by shortening games when the home team is closely ahead. As with the yellow cards, the mechanism is related to the crowd attending the game.

The continuous rules adjustments to ease the referee's job commonly hit the human facet where justice lacks systematic fairness. The inevitable, as Kahneman et al. (2021) would put it. Thus, the VAR is nothing else but an advanced technical toolkit to do what the soccer institutions have been attempting for well over a century. None of the theoretical approaches we have discussed can deal with the exogenous factors that an arbitrator confronts when facing the unique environment of a World Cup soccer match. Pressure stems from the crowds, the players, reporters, and an audience that reaches every corner of the planet. It is safe to say that a vast majority of referees intend to impart justice in the fairest possible way. Unlike in most situations depicted in the abundant literature on justice (whether reviewed here or not), whatever the decision, the debate can carry on for decades. This kind of pressure is beyond the typical argument in any theory of justice. Some, it is worth noting, have thought about intergenerational justice, which could be valid in this case. Still, there is no conclusive argument in how an arbitrator should act fairly when her decisions are challenged not only by the parties involved but potentially by millions who are rooting for one team or the other.

VAR, it turns out, is simply an instrument that follows on with the historic quest for justice, where the main difference is that the arbitrator is now composed of humans and machines. Such a quest is not unique to sports, but it is general to all activities where judgment is involved. To reduce variance (noise) in court decisions, the US government in the 1980s issued mandatory sentencing guidelines to restrict the range of criminal sentences (Kahneman et al., 2021). Soccer, of course, has its own guidelines. In soccer, however, interpretation is a crucial part of the decision process. But this is also true in a court. Critics of the guidelines arose because they were too rigid and did not allow the judge to consider the "complexities of each individual case" (Kahneman et al., 2021, p. 23). In the early twenty-first century, the guidelines became advisory rather than mandatory.

Soccer judges, referees, face the complexities of individual cases dozens of times in a soccer match, and they need to decide based on the set of rules in a short period of time. VAR is but a mechanical artifact to help referees in that complex process in some specific situations. The decisions remain ultimately humans with their strengths and flaws. The quest for justice, the pursuit of fairness, is not over.

References

Allingham, M. (2014). *Distributive justice*. Routledge.

Barry, B. (1989). *Theories of justice*. University of California Press.s

Binmore, K. (2009). *Fairness as a natural phenomenon*. http://else.econ.ucl.ac.uk/papers/uploaded/332.pdf. Accessed March 31, 2021.

Bryson, A., Dolton, P., Reade, J. J., Schreyer, D., & Singleton, C. (2021). Causal effects of an absent crowd on performances and refereeing decisions during Covid-19. *Economics Letters, 198*, 109664.

Buraimo, B., Forrest, D., & Simmons, R. (2010). The 12th man?: Refereeing bias in English and German soccer. *Journal of the Royal Statistical Society: Series A (Statistics in Society), 173*(2), 431–449.

De Soto, A. Q. F. (2015). *Goles y banderas: fútbol e identidades nacionales en España*. Marcial Pons Historia.

Garicano, L., Palacios-Huerta, I., & Prendergast, C. (2005). Favoritism under social pressure. *Review of Economics and Statistics, 87*(2), 208–216.

Harvey, A. (2005). *Football: The first hundred years: The untold story*. Psychology Press.

Hesse, U. (2003). *Tor!: The story of German football*. WSC Books Limited.

Goldblatt, D. (2007). *The ball is round: A global history of football*. Penguin UK.

Kahneman, D., Knetsch, J. L., & Thaler, R. H. (1986). Fairness and the assumptions of economics. *Journal of Business, 59*(S4), S285–S300.

Kahneman, D., Siboni, O., & Sunstein, C. (2021). *Noise: A flaw in human judgement*. Little Brown Spark.

Konow, J. (2003). Which is the fairest one of all? A positive analysis of justice theories. *Journal of Economic Literature, 41*(4), 1188–1239.

Moulin, H. (2004). *Fair division and collective welfare*. MIT Press.

Reid, I., & Zisserman, A. (1996, April). Goal-directed video metrology. In *European conference on computer vision* (pp. 647–658). Springer.

Scanlon, T. M. (1982). Contractualism and utilitarianism. In A. Sen & B. Williams (Eds.), *Utilitarianism and beyond*. Cambridge University Press.

Sen, A. K. (2009). *The idea of justice*. Harvard University Press.

Sen, A. (2017). Ethics and the foundation of global justice. *Ethics & International Affairs, 31*(3), 261–270.

Taylor, R., & Jamrich, K. (2018). Puskás sobre Puskás. Vida y gloria de una leyenda del fútbol. Ed. Corner.

Tovar, J. (2014). *Números redondos.* Grijalbo.

Tovar, J. (2021). Soccer, World War II and coronavirus: A comparative analysis of how the sport shut down. *Soccer & Society, 22*(1–2), 66–74. https://doi.org/10.1080/14660970.2020.1755270

Waine, A., & Naglo, K. (Eds.). (2013). *On and off the field: Football culture in England and Germany.* Springer Publishing House.

Wilson, J. (2013). *Inverting the pyramid: The history of soccer tactics.* Bold Type Books.

CHAPTER 3

The Debate of VAR

Abstract There are two significant innovations in soccer refereeing in the last decade. The history behind the approval of the goal-line technology and the video assistant referee allows the reader to understand the intrinsic difficulties in implementing new technologies in the conservative world of soccer. This chapter also reviews the relevant literature about the impact that the VAR has had on the sport. A thorough review of FIFA's official experiment to determine the validity of soccer gives way to recent papers showing that the VAR tends to reduce fouls and offside while increasing the minutes played.

Keyword FIFA World Cup Russia 2018 · FIFA World Cup France 2019 · Video Assistant Referee · Goal-line technology · Referee · Penalty

There are two significant innovations in soccer refereeing in the last decade. First came the introduction of the goal-line technology and then the VAR. The former, introduced in 2012, alerts the referee when the ball crosses the goal line. Controversies like Hurst's goal in 1966 or Lampard's disallowed goal in a similar situation in the 2010 World Cup

© The Author(s), under exclusive license to Springer Nature 29
Switzerland AG 2021
J. Tovar, *On Fairness, Justice, and VAR*,
Palgrave Pivots in Sports Economics,
https://doi.org/10.1007/978-3-030-84814-9_3

round of sixteen match between England and Germany are essentially a matter of the past in top leagues and international competitions. The latter potentially has a more profound impact on soccer because it is more invasive, and its use is more frequent than the goal-line technology.

THE HISTORY BEHIND THE VAR

During the 2005 IFAB Annual Meeting, Adidas and Cairos presented a new goal technology later tested at that year's Under 17 World Championship held in Peru and the Club World Cup. Despite some early proposals to implement the technology in the 2006 World Cup, FIFA's full approval would still take years. By 2006, the technology was being tested in Italy and England, but resistance was still strong two years later. During the 2008 IFAB meeting, Michel Platini, then UEFA President, and Ángel María Villar, President of the Spanish Soccer Federation and FIFA Vice President, were still expressing concerns about this technology. The conservative world of soccer has always been reluctant to change. This was no exception. According to the minutes of the 2008 meeting, concerns were raised that the use of "such technology would be contrary to the universality of the game" and that in time its use would expand beyond the goal line, for instance, "the penalty area."[1] On the universality of the game, one can but suspect that they were concerned about soccer evolution beyond the wealthiest leagues. If that is so, it is not clear why improving some without worsening others would be a wrong move. On the latter, they were right. Eventually, (a different) technology moved beyond the goal line.

Five years after the first presentation, and despite advances made by firms Adidas/Cairos and Hawk-Eye, using chip-in-ball technology the former, high-resolution cameras the latter, IFAB rejected not only the goal-line technology but "indeed technology in general within the game."[2] The conservative body rejected any innovations on the grounds of a negative impact on the essence of the game.

---

[1] Page 9 of the Minutes of the 2008 Annual General Meeting of the International Football Association Board available at https://static-3eb8.kxcdn.com/documents/816/131001_070819_2008_IFAB_AGM_Minutes.pdf, visited April 12, 2021.

[2] Page 15 of the Minutes of the 2010 Annual General Meeting of the International Football Association Board available at https://static-3eb8.kxcdn.com/documents/821/133133_070819_2010_IFAB_AGM_Minutes.pdf, visited April 12, 2021.

Everything changed in the 37th minute of the game between England and Germany in South Africa 2010. At 2–1 against, the English player Lampard shot from just outside the box. The ball, not very hard, passed over Neuer's final effort and hit the crossbar's underside. All too similar to what had happened in 1966. Capello, England's manager, celebrated on the sideline. Neither the Uruguayan referee, Jorge Larrionda, nor his assistant Mauricio Espinosa, saw that the ball had bounced behind the goal line. Unlike in 1966, the TV repetition was crystal clear. It was a goal by at least half a meter. FIFA's top executives, one can imagine, immediately recalled that meeting in Zurich in March 2010, just a few months before the World Cup's kick-off. The response was to commission some field tests in February 2011, which eventually led to the goal-line technology's approval in 2012. It had a condition, though. Such technology could only be applied to the goal line.

The decision made in 2012 was a significant step forward in football rule's management, but by no means was it a change in paradigm. During the 2013 IFAB meeting, there were concerns about the existence of monitoring systems available to teams, some even with the capacity to provide information in the technical area during a given match. Such circumstances were not new. Already in 2010, there were concerns and debates on banning the use of new technologies such as computers, tablets, and cellular phones within the technical area.

In the 2013 meeting, the concept of technology, as opposed to the pureness of soccer, was raised again, with FIFA's President Joseph Blatter stating that IFAB had already conceded one technology and that no other should be allowed. He noted that a chip in a jersey today could lead to a camera and eventually impact tactics driving the sport in the wrong direction. A year later, on this matter, at the IFAB meeting, there were concerns that they were running behind the reality of the game as many teams already used devices with detailed event-level data. Still, there were members against allowing the use of such devices.

In the 2013–2014 season, the Royal Dutch Football Association (KNVB) launched an initiative called Refereeing 2.0. Beyond trials to implement the FIFA-approved goal-line technology, they were interested in promoting technology to improve the quality of the game and raise the general acceptance of refereeing decisions. However, during IFAB's 2014 annual meeting, the consensus was that none but the goal-line technology should be accepted on the field and advised the KNVB against any pilot regarding video replay for match officials. Moreover, at the time, they agreed that there should be no further research into the use of any such technology.

Just a year later, there was a drastic change in the perception of technology. The KNVB turned a deaf ear to IFAB's recommendation and experimented with video footage provided b y broadcaster's cameras. Moreover, during the experiment, there was a separate room with the capacity to give the referee instantaneously additional information. It was called a video assistant. The seed for the use of VAR was in place.

By 2015, IFAB accepted this and other experiments to study the advantages and disadvantages of an instant video replay system. At the time, there remained concerns about impacting the universality of the game, but more troubling about changing "the game, with a possible diminution of the referee's authority as the video takes more influence." The latter could "result in an ever-increasing pressure on the referee from the spectators, players, and coaches."[3] One immediately thinks about the role of the arbitrator discussed in the previous section, which must be independent, knowledgeable, and fair, but who in soccer is exposed to tremendous pressure from many different angles. It also brings to mind the concern about machines replacing judges in US courts. If the judicial system introduced machines, as in soccer, it could have unintended consequences. Not surprisingly, during the VAR implementation process, these types of arguments popped up early.

The pace sped up as the soccer community pressed IFAB to approve an instant video replay mechanism. In the 2016 meeting, the discussion at IFAB focused on how to test such a system, and it made clear that the subject of assistance should only be for game-changing situations: (i) goals scored, (ii) penalty/no-penalty situations, and (iii) direct red cards. An advisory panel suggested that the system also considered cases where the players' identity was mistaken, and she had received a yellow or red card.

The response from soccer stakeholders was immediate. Australia, Brazil, Germany, Portugal, the Netherlands, and the United States agreed to participate in the experiment. After testing the system in December 2016's FIFA Club World Cup, IFAB authorized further experiments in 2017, leading to the VAR approval on the IFAB meeting held on March

---

[3] Page 13 of the Minutes of the 2015 Annual General Meeting of the International Football Association Board available at https://static-3eb8.kxcdn.com/documents/222/121321_240217_2015min.pdf, visited April 12, 2021.

3, 2018. A couple of weeks later, FIFA announced that Russia 2018 would be the first World Cup with a complete VAR system.

According to FIFA, during the 2018 World Cup, the VAR team consisted of a video assistant referee and three video assistant referees who support the referee from a centralized video operation room.[4] The team had access to 33 broadcast cameras, eight slow-motion and four super slow-motion plus two offside cameras. During the knockout stages, there were two additional ultra-slow-motion cameras behind each goal.

The VAR system operated similarly during the 2019 Women World Cup, with subtle differences. The VAR team consisted of a video assistant referee and two, instead of three video assistant referees. The FIFA website is not clear on how many cameras were available for the VAR team beyond the fact that most broadcaster cameras were available. Still, there were fewer available than for the male's competition.[5] VAR decisions followed Russia's 2018 protocols.

VAR Literature

There is a growing but still limited literature reviewing the operation of VAR in elite football. Most of the focus is on male soccer in some of the top European leagues. Historically, the most relevant paper to date is Spitz et al. (2021), the published version of the IFAB commissioned work to determine the impact and accuracy of the novel system. As detailed above, IFAB was reluctant to implement further innovations beyond the goal-line technology. However, mountain pressure led IFAB to approve a two-year experiment implemented by a team led by the University of Leuven. Although the results were reported in the March 2018 IFAB meeting, a full-length analysis was published a couple of years later by Spitz et al. (2021).

The paper was interested in understanding how the referee's decisions changed with VAR. To do so, they had the national referees committee in each of the thirteen participant countries evaluate each game situation independently. Next, considering events with VAR intervention, they used

---

[4] This information on the VAR operation during Russia 2018 was retrieved from FIFA´s official website: https://football-technology.fifa.com/en/innovations/var-at-the-world-cup/, visited April 14, 2021.

[5] The information is available at https://football-technology.fifa.com/en/innovations/var-at-the-womens-world-cup/, visited April 14, 2021.

their decision as a benchmark to statistically compare the referee's in-game initial ruling with the final decision. Note that in practice, they implemented a proxy for what Kahneman et al. (2021) denoted as a noise audit, an experiment designed to measure how much disagreement exists between professionals when dealing with similar cases.

The experiment took place between January 2017 and June 2018. The latter suggests that the reports presented at the March 2018 IFAB meeting were preliminary. Indeed, the Media Package released states that the analysis is based on 972 competitive (i.e., not friendly) matches, while Spitz et al. (2021) use data on 2195 competitive games.

A key feature with VAR is to improve fairness which, as already discussed, is a relative concept. Spitz et al. (2021) determined that they would only use unanimous decisions made by the national referee committee to compare decision accuracy. That is, between 5 and 10 referees had to agree on a given action. Out of 9,732 checks, 638 (6.5%) were discarded because of a lack of unanimity within the committees. The reported results show that out of the remaining 9,094 situations checked, the referee's initial decision was accurate 92.1% of the time. Once VAR intervened, accuracy increased to 98.3%.

The results are promising, but they deserve a deeper look. 92% and 98% accuracy seem high. However, controversies are not built on unanimous decisions. Consider the 1990 World Cup final between Germany and Argentina, arguably the ugliest final ever seen. The Germans won thanks to a late penalty kick scored by Brehme. In the 84th minute, Sensini, the Argentinian defender, jostled Völler, the German striker. Codesal, the Mexican referee, immediately called the penalty kick. A unanimously controversial decision. Sensini, approaching Völler from his left, stretched his right leg as much as possible while the German protects the ball with his body. Völler falls, as did the Argentinian. Sensini never touches the ball, but it is not clear that his legs touched the contender. His right arm, though, slides past Völler's back, and it is then, when the striker feels the defender's movement, that he falls or dives, depending on who tells the story. Thirty years later, Codesal argued that the "defender does not touch the ball, although he was trying to play it. He contacts the striker with his thigh, and the waist with his forearm. Thus, he falls."[6]

---

[6] https://www.infobae.com/america/deportes/2020/07/08/codesal-exclusivo-a-30-anos-de-la-polemica-final-de-italia-90-el-analisis-de-sus-sanciones-su-enojo-con-maradona-y-la-ultima-amenaza-que-recibio/, visited April 15, 2021.

The New York Times called it a "somewhat dubious" penalty call.[7] *El Mundo Deportivo*, the Spanish sports newspaper, said it was "at least doubtful."[8] As noted above, it is not overstating that it was a unanimously controversial decision.

In Scanlon's terms, Codesal has a strong desire to justify his actions on the grounds that others could not reasonably reject them. However, as Scanlon (1982) notes, people are willing to go considerable lengths to avoid admitting the unjustifiability of their actions. Indeed, two other potential penalty kicks were also highly controversial during that game. With the game still tied, a German cross, right to left, found Augenthaler seven feet from the goal line, having Goycoechea, the Argentinian goalkeeper, as the only opposition between him and glory. Augenthaler entered the six-yard box as the keeper narrowed the angle by sliding on his knees. With the goalkeeper upon him, the German pulled the ball to his right, and before he could follow it, Goycoechea, still kneeling, raised his knees slightly as a necessary movement to get up and follow the ball. During that almost imperceptible movement, he touches and knocks Augenthaler. A penalty kick, among others, for *El Mundo Deportivo*.[9] The referee's decision is even more questionable, given that he was just one meter away.

During that World Cup, intentionality played a role. Codesal claimed that Goycoechea's contact with Augenthaler was unintentional; thus, he could not call the penalty kick. A curious argument when recalling Völler's penalty because there is little doubt that Sensini's objective was the ball.

In a 2006 interview for the Spanish newspaper *El País*, Andreas Brehme said that Völler's struggle with Sensini was not a penalty. However, he claimed, "there was a penalty earlier." He was, of course, referring to Goycoechea's foul on Augenthaler.[10]

Had this been all, having Germany won, the controversy would be historically negligible. However, in the 78th minute, there was a tackle

---

[7] https://www.nytimes.com/1990/07/09/sports/sports-of-the-times-winning-ugly-losing-ugly-just-plain-ugly.html, visited April 15, 2021.

[8] http://hemeroteca.mundodeportivo.com/preview/1990/07/09/pagina-4/1221555/pdf.html, visited April 15, 2021.

[9] Idem.

[10] https://elpais.com/diario/2006/06/15/deportes/1150322419_850215.html, visited April 15, 2021.

from Matthäus to Calderón inside the German penalty area. A German defender headed away following a corner kick, but the ball rose too high and fell still inside the box. Despite his talent, Matthäus could not control the ball with the necessary precision, which went long, just to the right corner of the box. Gabriel Humberto Calderon took the ball, Matthäus, trying to regain control of the ball, rushed past the Argentinian who, a second later, abruptly fell. There was never any replay, and the existing tape was unclear. However, in May 2020, Calderón tweeted unseen footage, at least in the West, from an Asian broadcaster.[11] The new footage shows the play as Codesal must have seen it. Matthäus left foot, while passing by, drags the Argentinian left foot in two successive movements. The first one touches Calderón's ankle, but not enough to make him fall. However, as Calderón attempts to move forward, searching for the ball, Matthäus again touches his rival's ankle, whose left foot is a few centimeters in the air. The German trips Calderón, but no penalty was called. Minutes later, Codesal would point the penalty spot in the Argentinian box.

Situations like the ones Codesal had to face in 1990 are the typical noisy events. It probably has some similarity to the 638 checks discarded by Spitz et al. (2021). Their approach, in practice, strips the experiment from the noise component, a critical factor in understanding the relevance of disagreement in the game. The high accuracy rate is undoubtedly biased when discarding contentious situations. When a panel of referees is unable to reach a verdict, it is apparent that there is no universal acceptance of any final decision, even with VAR. The 90% + accuracy rate seems overstated, as controversial decisions remain, even if the evidence in general quantitatively supports VAR's implementation.

Indeed, VAR experiments run elsewhere support the general high accurate findings, but they reinforce the doubts about its limitations when dealing with controversial decisions. In the German Bundesliga, which ran live experiments during the 2017/2018 season, there were 1,870 double check situations, 1,321 of which involved no communication with the referee. In 461 cases, VAR confirmed the referee's initial call, plus there were 88 interventions where the VAR recommended changing the initial call. Sixty-four initially wrong calls were overturned by VAR, which also wrongly judged 14 situations (Kolbinger, 2019). The low

---

[11] https://twitter.com/gabihcalderon/status/1259839341473529858/, visited April 15, 2021.

rate of the VAR's effect in decision changes replicates using Spanish data where match-changing incidents led to no review in 70% of the matches (Lago-Peñas et al., 2020).

In Italy, as in Germany, several tests preceded VAR's implementation in Serie A for the 2017/2018 season. During that period, and out of 2,023 situations, 117 were changed, although there is no way to determine whether VAR made any miscalls (Simón, 2019).

The Major League Soccer (MLS), not surprisingly given the tradition in other US professional sports, was an early VAR adopter. Five matches used VAR as soon as 2016. During the first half of the 2017 season, the VAR tests led to its full adoption for the second half. Unlike in Europe, the results were not benign with referees. Three out of four VAR reviews, 104 out of 140, were overturned (Warren, 2019). Such a high rate may be related to the American culture, where VAR may be novel to soccer, but not to their sporting culture, or simply that referees are not doing a great job. I tend to sympathize with the former because there is no shame in calling any mistakes the referee can make in their culture. In Europe, VAR officials might feel that any correction on judgments made can potentially undermine the referee's authority. That is not true in the United States.

For the most part, the subsequent available literature focuses on the VAR's effects in the game. The results are robust across countries when reviewing evidence from the Chinese Super League (Han et al., 2020), the Italian Serie A, and German Bundesliga (Lago-Peñas et al., 2019) and Spain (Lago-Peñas et al., 2020). Maybe surprisingly, the results are also very similar when comparing data between the 2014 and the 2018 World Cup (Kubayi et al., 2021).

A common finding is a reduction in the number of offsides and fouls, the latter not true for the Spanish league (Han et al., 2020; Lago-Peñas et al., 2019, 2020) or the World Cup (Kubayi et al., 2021). An increase in the playing time is also true for the three leagues, but there seems to be no effect in the second half in Italy and Germany. Errekagorri et al. (2020), using data for Spain, find a slightly positive correlation between the use of VAR per game and the number of minutes played, but a decrease in the effective time played when comparing the use of VAR once in a game with no VAR use. Kubayi et al. (2021) report an increase in playing time in Russia 2018 relative to Brazil 2014 for total playing time and the first and second half. The number of yellow cards fell in Serie A and the Bundesliga (Lago-Peñas et al, 2019; Simón, 2019).

In other indicators, home team advantage decreased in China (Han et al., 2020) and protest, diving, and unsporting conduct in Spain (Simón, 2019). Errekagorri et al. (2020) find some week evidence that the total distance covered by players might have increased and that goals increased with VAR.

Overall, there is conflicting evidence about the precision of the referees' decisions. European data tends to support the referees, while US data suggests otherwise. However, the VAR technology is relatively accurate, but there remains a non-negligible number of controversial events. The literature available has described a reduction in fouls and offsides, which a common cause cannot explain. The latter seems pretty straightforward: referees tend to rely on the VAR technology and do not need to sanction an offside if in doubt because it is very easy to rectify if it ends up in a goal. If, on the contrary, they mistakenly call an offside, there is no way to repair the mistake.

It is not obvious how to explain the reduction in fouls. The VAR will not call a foul, except if it is inside the box. Maybe it is just a psychological effect, and referees simply rely more on the technology, thus calling fewer fouls unconsciously. On the other hand, perhaps players are aware that any misconduct has bigger chances of detection.

References

Errekagorri, I., Castellano, J., Echeazarra, I., & Lago-Peñas, C. (2020). The effects of the video assistant referee system (VAR) on the playing time, technical-tactical and physical performance in elite soccer. *International Journal of Performance Analysis in Sport, 20*(5), 808–817.

Han, B., Chen, Q., Lago-Peñas, C., Wang, C., & Liu, T. (2020). The influence of the video assistant referee on the Chinese Super League. *International Journal of Sports Science & Coaching, 15*(5–6), 662–668.

Kahneman, D., Siboni, O., & Sunstein, C. (2021). *Noise: A flaw in human judgement*. Little Brown Spark.

Kolbinger, O. (2019). VAR experiments in the Bundesliga. In M. Armenteros, A. J. Benítez, & M. A. Betancor (Eds.), *The use of video technologies in refereeing football and other sports*. Taylor & Francis.

Kubayi, A., Larkin, P., & Toriola, A. (2021). The impact of video assistant referee (VAR) on match performance variables at men's FIFA World Cup tournaments. *Proceedings of the Institution of Mechanical Engineers, Part P: Journal of Sports Engineering and Technology*. https://doi.org/10.1177/175433712 1997581.

Lago-Peñas, C., Ezequiel, R., & Anton, K. (2019). How does video assistant referee (VAR) modify the game in elite soccer? *International Journal of Performance Analysis in Sport, 19*(4), 646–653.

Lago-Peñas, C., Gómez, M. A., & Pollard, R. (2020). The effect of the video assistant referee on referee's decisions in the Spanish LaLiga. *International Journal of Sports Science & Coaching.* https://doi.org/10.1177/174795412 0980111.

Scanlon, T. M. (1982). Contractualism and utilitarianism. In A. Sen & B. Williams (Eds.), *Utilitarianism and beyond*. Cambridge University Press.

Simón, J. A. (2019). VAR experiments in the Italian Serie A League. In M. Armenteros, A. J. Benítez, & M. A. Betancor (Eds.), *The use of video technologies in refereeing football and other sports*. Taylor & Francis.

Spitz, J., Wagemans, J., Memmert, D., Williams, A. M., & Helsen, W. F. (2021). Video assistant referees (VAR): The impact of technology on decision making in association football referees. *Journal of Sports Sciences, 39*(2), 147–153.

Warren, C. (2019). VAR experiments in major league soccer (MLS). In M. Armenteros, A. J. Benítez, & M. A. Betancor (Eds.), *The use of video technologies in refereeing football and other sports*. Taylor & Francis.

CHAPTER 4

VAR in Russia 2018 and France 2019

Abstract This chapter uses detailed event-level data to determine and review every VAR intervention during the men's 2018 and the women's 2019 World Cup. Quantitatively, it examines the number of interventions, the causes, and outcomes of the VAR, as well as the referee's decision changes. It also checks the impact on the number of minutes played, on referee's and when and why it was not used. Although VAR has, statistically, a very high accuracy rate (whose definition is debatable), a qualitative review of its use, using both current and past events, suggests that controversy remains significant even when using the new technology.

Keyword Video Assistant Referee · Yellow cards · Red Cards · Event-level data · Noise · Experiment

The VAR technology debuted during the FIFA World Cup held in Russia in 2018. The instrument, as discussed earlier, was approved just a few months before the World Cup. The first time necessarily requires some adaptation. Consider yellow and red cards, first introduced in Mexico in 1970. Players have been sent off since Uruguay 1930, when the Peruvian Galindo was sent off in the game that his team lost against Romania. Cards, however, were not used until the Mexican World Cup, with a total

© The Author(s), under exclusive license to Springer Nature
Switzerland AG 2021
J. Tovar, *On Fairness, Justice, and VAR*,
Palgrave Pivots in Sports Economics,
https://doi.org/10.1007/978-3-030-84814-9_4

of fifty-eight yellow cards awarded during the tournament. Just four years later, in Germany in 1974, with the same number of teams competing, sixteen, eighty-seven times the referees showed a yellow card. No player saw a red card during the 1970 cup. Four years later, in Germany, during the inaugural match between the host and Chile, the South American Caszely was ejected after fouling Berti Vogts. A total of five players saw the red card during the German World Cup.

The figures on yellow and red cards suggest that using a new instrument might be limited when implemented for the first time. Although the VAR was used previously in some soccer matches before Russia, the 2018 World Cup was its planetary debut. Given the scale of the male World Cup and the relative novelty of the technology, its use might have some biases that only time will allow to detect. However, another major event took place just a year later, the female World Cup in France. The use of data from both tournaments gives a comprehensive overview of the deployment of VAR.

The Men's World Cup had 32 teams and 64 games, while 24 teams played 52 games in the Female's version. When interpreting the aggregate descriptive data, one must keep this in mind. To establish the use of VAR, I use event-level data compiled by OPTA and provided by www. golyfutbol.com. The analytics company continuously follows the ball and records each use of the VAR.

As a technical note, it is worth remarking that the VAR makes capturing the event-level data somewhat messy because, given its nature, there is the need to add or review some events *ex-post*. For instance, an initially recorded goal might be canceled, or a goal assist can change to an offside pass. OPTA includes some qualifiers in VAR interventions that facilitate detecting the relevant events out of 188,639 between the matches held in Russia and France. Upon further and detailed analysis of the data, some events were classified as contentious referee decisions but not explicitly as VAR interventions. I catalog four of these events as VAR interventions after reviewing video footage, numerous chronicles, and live web feeds of each relevant game.[1]

---

[1] Video footage is available in youtube.com. Live feeds typically reviewed came from The Guardian (UK), AS (Spain), El Mundo Deportivo (Spain), Futbolred (Colombia), plus chronicles from El Pais (Spain) and the New York Times (United States) among other relevant websites.

Table 4.1 VAR interventions

World cup	Decision Cancelled	Decision Confirmed	Total
France 2019	28	9	37
Russia 2018	16	6	22
Total	44	15	59

Source Opta. Own calculations

On the other hand, the richness of the data allows for a detailed review of the reasons to use VAR and the outcome of the process. Moreover, a careful cleaning process of the dataset, including the revision of video footage and live feeds, allows determining with great precision the time spent in each VAR event. Thus, it is possible to establish how many minutes and seconds the referee spent deciding for each type of event.

A natural limitation of the data available is that it only considers events where the referee publicly stopped the game because there is no information on internal talks which might have taken place between the game's officials. Likewise, there is no way to know the use of VAR in the video room. Still, given that these activities are not public, they must have little effect on players, fans, and media behavior.

VAR Interventions in the World Cup

During the combined World Cups, there were 59 VAR interventions (Table 4.1). France 2019 saw over 70% more VAR interventions despite having fewer games than those registered during Russia 2018, 37 vs. 22.

These numbers do not match FIFA's official figures. In Russia 2018, there were officially 455 incidents, including twenty VAR reviews called, seventeen of which canceled the decision, and three confirmed it.[2] Using these numbers, FIFA concludes that the match-changing decision accuracy is 95.6% correct without VAR and 99.35% when VAR changed seventeen wrong decisions. The former results from dividing 435 (subtracting the twenty VAR reviews calls out of the total number of incidents) by 455. The latter takes away just the three VAR confirmed decisions. It is not clear that these indicators imply match decision accuracy because they

[2] Available at https://www.fifa.com/worldcup/news/the-2018-fifa-world-cuptm-in-numbers. Visited May 4, 2021.

implicitly infer that VAR is correct in the 435 decisions not reviewed and when changing a decision. This assumption is strong because the strategy followed does not allow to determine if, in fact, the decisions changed or not reviewed were correct.

Table 4.1's figures also differ from FIFA's official numbers for France 2019. FIFA reports 535 incidents checked, including thirty-three VAR reviews.[3] It suggests that referees were more prone to use the VAR technology in France relative to Russia, potentially because of reasons discussed earlier.

According to FIFA, VAR led to twenty-nine decisions changed and four confirmations leading to a tremendous match-changing decisions accuracy rate. However, they are not reported, maybe because, as noted above, they are not transparent indicators.

One would wish to have a complete match between FIFA's figures and OPTA data. The discrepancies mostly have to do with the interpretation of a VAR intervention. FIFA calls them VAR reviews, some of which are "on-field reviews," the other "only VAR reviews." The former is when the referee looks at the replay footage in the referee review area. These are straightforward to catch because the referee physically announces that she will personally check the contentious event. The latter, however, when the referee communicates with the VAR room using the earpiece, is not as evident.

The methodology to determine VAR reviews in what follows is based on OPTA's data and the referee explicitly stopping the game for some contentious decision. There is no publicly available data on the hundreds of communications that FIFA reports the referee having with the VAR room, only on decisions visible to reporters, fans, and broadcasters. The annex reports the VAR reviews used in the analysis that follows. It includes data on the match, the reason for the intervention, the decision, the outcome, and the team that benefited.

FIFA's data coincides with Table 4.1 in reporting more reviews per game in France than in Russia. Their data, including all visible and non-visible VAR checks, implies 10.28 reviews per match, forty-four percent higher than during Russia 2018, when there were only 7.1 checks per game.

---

[3] Available at https://img.fifa.com/image/upload/zeghumlzve8t7pppcw8m.pdf. Visited May 4 2021.

The excess in VAR interventions during the 2019 World Cup can be attributed at least to two factors. First, as already discussed, the novelty of the mechanism in Russia 2018.The use of VAR was widely reviewed by the media during that World Cup, potentially (maybe unconsciously) limiting the referees and the video assistant referees in its use concerned for being in the eye of the hurricane. In contrast, by 2019, when the Female World Cup took place, VAR had a history, albeit short.

However, at the time of the French World Cup, no senior women's domestic or international competition had ever used VAR; thus, although aware of VAR, there was a limited experience in its use. Adding that all referees, assistant referees, and video assistant referees were women, the VAR was, in practice, a novelty for both players and officials. Still, the previous experience of VAR i n men's competitions worldwide made the instrument relatively common knowledge, definitely not an absolute novelty as had been in 2018.

A second potential explanation for the difference in the number of VAR interventions in Russia relative to France might be that male soccer and female soccer are structurally different. With no pretensions of settling such a complex debate, a proxy for that hypothesis is the number of fouls, passes, and shots taken during each game.

Figure 4.1 depicts the distribution for passes, fouls, and shots in each World Cup. The shadowed area represents all observations between the 25th and 75th percentile, with the darker horizontal line indicating the median. The size of the shaded regions is similar across World Cups, suggesting that the distribution is not that different between male and female top soccer matches.

There is, nevertheless, evidence that male football is faster, if measured by the number of passes, and more aggressive when looking at fouls. Indeed, the mean difference between male and female World Cup passes and fouls is statistically significant.[4] Shots, on the other hand, are similar and not statistically different.

Combining the higher number of fouls in Russia 2018 with the constrained use of VAR reinforces the point where its use was not sought by referees as much as it was in 2019. Beyond the novelty or not of the VAR and the potential differences between male and female soccer, it may also matter the level of exposure that referees in the Russia 2018

---

[4] The p-value of a t-test is 0.0003 for passes and 0.0000 for fouls.

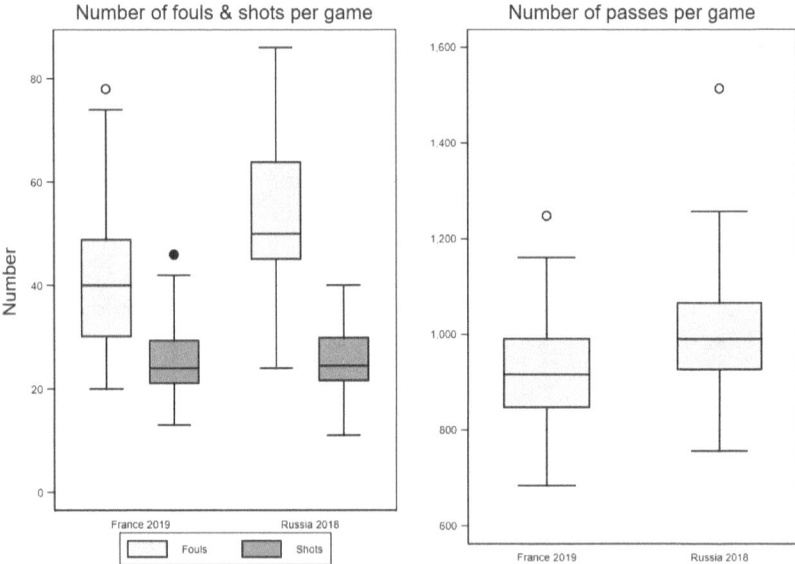

Fig. 4.1 Russia 2018 vs France 2019: Events (*Source* Opta. Own calculations)

Word Cup had relative to their counterparts in France 2019. According to FIFA, 3.2 billion people watched the 2018 male version, almost three times that of France 2019: 1.12 billion. In addition, the final match in France 2019 had 260 million viewers, while the male final had 1.12 billion.[5] However, in practice, it is not apparent that an individual will react significantly differently when knowing that a billion people will question her decisions relative to one that will be monitored by a quarter billion. It follows that the relatively extensive use of VAR in France might be related to the better knowledge and understanding of the instrument.

Figure 4.2 depicts the reasons for the VAR interventions, another proxy to explore the use of the mechanism and potential differences between the male and female cups.

---

[5] According to FIFA website visited May 8th, 2021. https://www.fifa.com/womens worldcup/news/fifa-women-s-world-cup-2019tm-watched-by-more-than-1-billion,   and https://www.fifa.com/worldcup/news/more-than-half-the-world-watched-record-bre aking-2018-world-cup.

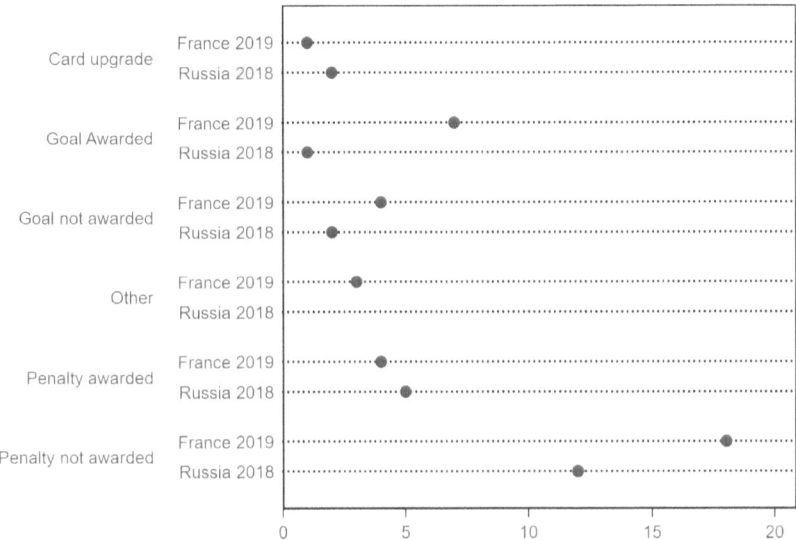

Fig. 4.2 VAR, number of interventions: reasons (*Source* Opta. Own calculations)

The most common reason to use the new technology in both World Cups was when a referee denied a penalty kick. The figure for the female World Cup is over 50% larger than in its male counterpart cup. There are also significant differences in goals awarded and in "others." The latter refers to three missed penalty kicks that the referee ordered to repeat because, upon reviewing the VAR, she concluded that the goalkeeper had none of her feet over the goal line. There was no such situation in Russia 2018.

The illegal movement of the goalkeeper did not come without controversy, particularly in the exciting match between Scotland and Argentina when the former lost a three-goal lead. The third goal for the Argentinians came when the referee pointed the spot in the last minute once reviewing the VAR. The Argentinian striker missed the shot but, VAR once again, called for its repetition because the goalkeeper moved a few inches forward before the shot; thus, none of her feet were over the line. Former US soccer star Hope Solo questioned the rule, but not the VAR itself, arguing that stepping over the line "does not do enough to cut down the angle during a penalty to justify a retake."[6] But the rule requires the goalkeeper to have at least one foot over the goal line, although one could discuss how much forward they can move before a retake is justified because of the narrowed angle. As shown extensively earlier, rules are dynamic, and although currently, goalkeepers must have a foot over the line, they could advance until the six-yard line in the early days. In that sense, Solo is right that history has given an advantage to the striker. Maybe it is unfair to the goalkeeper, but given that the objective is to score goals, it seems fair to the game. One might question the use of VAR in this situation because it is not clear that having the goalkeeper move in advance was one of the precepts under which VAR should operate but, still, goals/no-goals situations require the new technology. However, these types of cases (with a no-goal outcome) could lead to its use in no-goal shots, broadening the debate. It may well be this fuzzy area in which this event moves that led OPTA to call it "other."

The above simply proves that penalties are among the most controversial events in the game and seems like a perfect fit to use VAR with little margin for error. The World Cup history is full of controversies involving penalty kicks being the 2010 quarterfinal match between Paraguay and Spain among the most remembered because of the referee Carlos Batres's decisions.

With a nil-nil draw, Pique held for way too long Cardozo inside the box leading to a penalty. Cardozo shot to the left of Spanish goalkeeper Iker Casillas, who easily corralled the ball. The game moved on. The referee called a penalty kick a minute later, which came, according to Marca, the Spanish sports newspaper, after Villa "dived."[7] There are open controversies in both penalty kicks.

When Cardozo shoots for Paraguay, the referee should have repeated the penalty kick for two reasons. First, none of Casillas's legs were over the goal line. Second, three Spanish players were inside the box. The latter is particularly relevant because, in the other box, Batres ordered the repetition of Xabi Alonso's goal as at least one Spanish player was inside the box when he shot.

[6] https://edition.cnn.com/2019/06/20/football/womens-world-cup-var-spt-intl/index.html visited May 12, 2021.

[7] https://www.marca.com/marcador/futbol/2010/mundial/cuartos/par_spa/asilovivimos.html visited June 11, 2021.

In his second attempt, Xabi changed sides shooting to the left of Villar, who this time stopped the ball. However, unable to cage the ball, Villar lunged towards the edge of the six-yard box. Cesc, the Spanish midfielder, reached the ball a second earlier but went down under the challenge of Villar. It was an undeniable penalty kick.

In a matter of minutes, the Guatemalan referee made two game-changing mistakes. Three if, indeed, Villa dived. In soccer, two errors favoring different teams do not average to zero; instead, they add up. Had Batres had access to the VAR technology, maybe fairness had prevailed. The referee was unfair, but no one can certify who he harmed the most. In situations like this, there is a large window of opportunity for VAR. Solo's request to allow goalkeepers to leap forward is a matter of reviewing the social contract, depending on what the soccer community believes is just.

The dataset is rich enough to check beyond the causes and explore the outcome of the decisions. Figure 4.3 shows that, by far, the most common decision was to award a penalty kick, again with a difference in favor of France 2019.

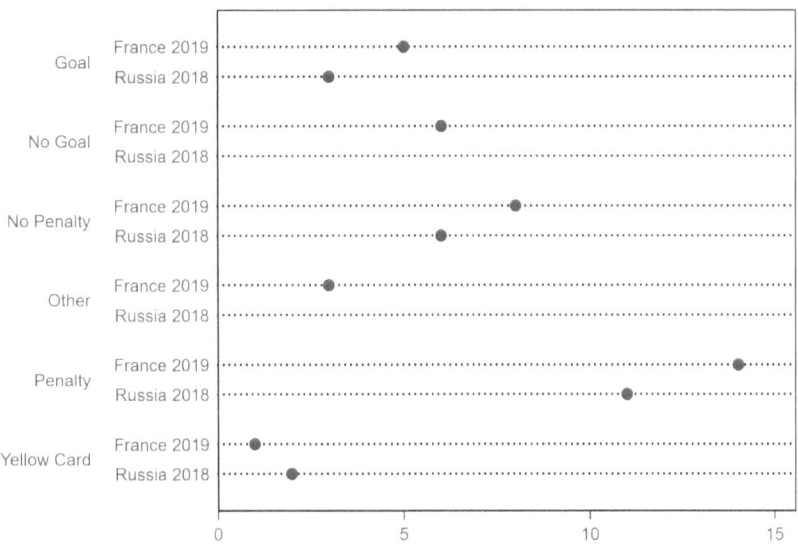

Fig. 4.3 VAR outcome (*Source* Opta. Own calculations)

The other noticeable feature of Fig. 4.3 is the no-goal outcome, only available in France 2019. A significant ruling occurred during the France vs. Brazil round of sixteen match. Just to the edge of the six-yard line, a cross from the right had Brazil goalkeeper, Barbara, rushing to the ball simultaneously with France's Valérie Gauvin, who was trying to head for goal. The Brazilian extends her arms to grab the ball while Gauvin was jumping for the header. Inevitable, they collide while in the air as the ball, which Barbara never fully caught, bounces on Gauvin's left shoulder while closing her eyes and enters smoothly into the goal. The French, note, touched the ball first and then bumped into the goalkeeper.

Although both the goalkeeper and the striker required medical assistance, the referee did not check the VAR for two minutes. It was not until the players had recovered that the referee decided to go and check the VAR. The whole process took over four minutes, the lengthiest VAR stoppage of both World Cups. France won the match in extra time with a delay because of the referee's decision, which can be controversial and points out one of the criticisms to VAR: the time necessary to make a decision.

The analysis so far is helpful to understand what drove the referee, but it says little about the dynamics of the process. Figure 4.4 depicts the transition between the reason for using VAR and its outcome. It is common, for instance, to concede a penalty when it was initially not awarded. Similarly, it is relatively frequent to cancel the decision having ruled a penalty kick.

VAR cancels numerous referees' decisions, whether in the male or the female World Cup. Under the (strong) assumption that the technology is always correct, the VAR is a success because out of 59 interventions; it corrected 74% of human mistakes.

The most common correction corresponds to penalties not awarded. It turned the referee's decision on thirteen occasions in France and nine in Russia. That represents 72% of penalties not awarded in 2019 and 75% in 2018.

The VAR had a visible effect on the number of penalty kicks awarded in both World Cups. There were twenty-eight penalties officially awarded during Russia 2018, a historical record. Officially in the sense that they effectively became a goal opportunity. Nine of these calls were initially not awarded, making it nineteen penalties awarded directly by referees during the World Cup. Additionally, VAR canceled three initially awarded penalty kicks. Thus, adding the nineteen penalty kicks that became a goal

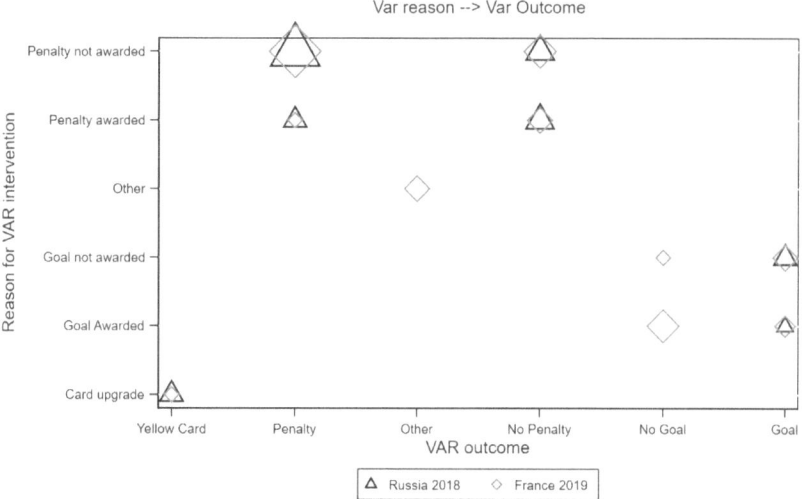

Fig. 4.4 Transition matrix: Russia 2018 & France 2019 (*Note* The size of the corresponding shape is positively correlated with the number of times a combination reason/outcome happens)

chance and the three overruled, the referees directly called twenty-two penalty kicks. That is a significantly larger number of penalties than the thirteen awarded in Brazil 2014 and the fifteen in South Africa 2010. Not surprisingly, Kubayi et al. (2021) find that the awarded penalties in Russia 2018 are statistically larger than those observed in Brasil 2014. In fact, since France 1998 when, as in Russia, 32 teams played the World Cup, there were never more than fifteen penalty kicks awarded. In Germany 2006, there were only five. Therefore, one can claim that twenty-two penalty kicks are by themselves a statistical outlier; twenty-eight is an exaggeration.

Replicating the exercise for the 2019 World Cup, the referees awarded 21 penalty kicks, thirteen of which were initially not awarded. Counting the three canceled calls adds to sixteen penalty kicks in the 52 games. In this case, the numbers do not differ much from the twenty-two penalties awarded in the previous World Cup held in 2015 in Canada. It does, however, significantly differ with the number of penalty kicks awarded in Germany 2011 and China 2007 when referees pointed to the spot four and eight times, respectively.

The large number of penalty kicks awarded in Russia and France suggests that the VAR influenced how the referees handled the games. Moreover, one can imagine that penalties with no VAR intervention probably did confirm the referee's call, but there is no public record on that. Still, the penalty kick is, arguably, the most extreme punishment and the most gratifying reward for any team. The history of the most recent World Cups suggests that the referees tend to be wary of pointing the spot when they lack certainty, but not as much as in previous tournaments. Even so, there has been plenty of controversy as Codesal's decisions in the 1990 final shows. A plausible interpretation is that referees feel less pressure when calling (or not calling) a penalty kick because they rely on the VAR to verify their decision. In that sense, VAR is a positive addition to the game because, with diminished pressure, they will try to impart justice more fairly, even if they are doing it unconsciously.

There is less excitement in analyzing the other causes for the VAR intervention (Fig. 4.4). Card upgrades are minimal, and we have already discussed penalty repetitions. In Russia 2018, the VAR only intervened to confirm one goal awarded, and it canceled the decisions on two goals not awarded. In France 2019, the controversy lies in the excessive use of VAR technology.

Consider the round of sixteen match between England and Cameroon, which saw too much VAR, up to four times. In a very aggressive game, the referee awarded an initially disallowed goal; she disallowed an initially validated goal, upgraded a card, and confirmed a no-penalty call. Three of those decisions were against the African team. The first VAR decision came after England's second goal, which video footage shows the scorer onside. However, the Cameroonians strongly disagreed with the decision, and all eleven players confronted the referee. An uncommon sight in modern times World Cups. Later, they refused to play, following their goal denied by an offside. Maybe too much VAR can generate chaos, although one must admit that the Africans disagreed since the first intervention.

It remains to check qualitatively if the VAR is an actual improvement over human decisions. It is too long and maybe boring to discuss every case, but using a series of examples, some of which we have already presented, we can generate a picture of what VAR brought to soccer in the summers of 2018 and 2019.

The first use of VAR in Russia 2018 was during the opening Group C match between Australia and France. A common complaint about VAR is that slow-motion tends to exaggerate movements, and contacts that have been normal for over a century become determinant. In fact, in Spitz et al.'s (2021) experiment, they only used slow-motion video to determine ball out of play (including goal/no-goal), point of contact for physical offenses, and handball. They used normal speed to decide if a handball was deliberate or the intensity of an offense. However, FIFA's 2018/2019 rules of the game simply state that VAR checks should "in general" follow the noted characterization.[8]

Reviewing in slow-motion, the replay of a given action leads to biases (Caruso et al. 2016, Spitz et al., 2018; Sperl et al., 2021). Caruso et al. (2016), using real-life surveillance footage, find that slow-motion can cause viewers to perceive an increase in intentionality. The slow-motion video makes viewers feel like the offender had more time to act, despite the fact that they are aware of the real-time elapsed. Spitz et al. (2018) had 88 elite referees from five different countries to review 60 different foul-play situations from international matches. The referees saw some cases in regular speed, others in slow-motion. The penalization for the latter was more severe than for the former.

The literature has followed several approaches to offset the bias. Using an experimental setting, Caruso et al. (2016) conclude that showing the viewer the same footage at regular speed can mitigate, though not elim-inate, the slow-motion bias. Assuming that the bias exists because the viewer underestimates the factor by which the video is slowed down, Sperl et al. (2021) explicitly displayed information about the speed of the video on the screen. They find that when the viewer is aware of the velocity of the slow-motion, the bias, defined here as the overestimation of the time that originally elapsed during the respective action, disappears. The slow-motion video bias is evidently troubling for VAR technology. It is suggestive of some potential adjustments, which we will discuss later on.

Going back to the opening Group C match in Russia 2018, Griez-mann, the French star, fell inside the area following a challenge by Risdon. The Uruguayan referee Cunha initially played on but, upon reviewing the VAR, pointed to the penalty spot.

Griezmann runs for the ball while entering the box. Risdon slid from behind, failing with his right foot to reach the ball. While still sliding, Griezmann drove forward the ball with his left foot. In his effort, but

---

[8] Fifa Rules of the Game, 2018/2019 available at https://img.fifa.com/image/upload/khhloe2xoigyna8juxw3.pdf visited May 26 2021.

having missed the ball, Risdon raises his right leg about two inches from the ground. At that point, interpretation kicks in.

In my view, he misses Griezmann's right leg, but because the French is running, Risdon slightly touches his ankle from behind. Upon feeling the touch, Griezmann falls (or dives). The UK Independent called it a "controversial first use of VAR."[9] The French L'Equipe called it a "doubtful but real contact" between the two players.[10] The Spanish AS sports newspaper wrote that it is difficult to judge if Griezmann's fall was "by inertia or voluntarily."[11]

The first experience with the VAR technology in a World Cup did not generate consensus. It would not be the last. In a decisive game, in the final matchday of Russia's Group B, Portugal and Iran played for a spot in the knockout stage. Trailing by one goal, already into injury time, following a cross from the right, the Iranian Sardar Azmoun and the Portuguese Cedric met in an aerial duel inside the box. The former headed downwards, and while still in the air, the ball hit Cedric's arm, naturally extended to balance the body. After the corresponding VAR check, the referee pointed the spot, and Iran drew the game. Insufficient for them, but enough to make Portugal lose the group's first place. The New York Times wrote that "this type of incidental contact is almost never called a penalty," while ESPN said it was a "controversial injury-time penalty."[12] Once again, there was no consensus.

Many of the referees' actions are questioned, not only when they opt for a particular decision but also when they ignore events that a majority believe they should have seen. Such happened in Group F's last matchday in the French World Cup with the United States and Sweden competing for first place. In the second half, minute 50, a cross from left t o ight reached Heath; wide opened just outside the box. She faced Jonna Andersson, moved left but came out right, shooting with barely an angle. The

[9] https://www.independent.co.uk/sport/football/world-cup/world-cup-2018-var-controversial-moments-a8445606.html visited May 11, 2020.

[10] https://www.lequipe.fr/Football/Actualites/La-france-souffre-mais-bat-l-australie-pour-son-entree-dans-la-coupe-du-monde/911940 visited May 11, 2021.

[11] https://as.com/futbol/2018/06/16/mundial/1529151248_557218.html, visited May 11, 2020.

[12] https://www.nytimes.com/2018/06/25/sports/world-cup/portugal-vs-iran-ronaldo.html visited May 13, 2021.
https://www.espn.com/soccer/report?gameId=498167 visited May 13, 2021.

ball, deflected by the Swedish defender, passed buzzing by the goal-keeper's head. The two-goal difference for the United States effectively closed the game.

However, when the ball was crossing, Carli Lloyd, the American forward, was offside. The footage is apparent. The New York Times and Time magazine both mentioned a possible offside.[13] Nevertheless, the referee awarded the goal, maybe interpreting that Lloyd did not interfere in the cross, which is hardly true. The ball reached Heath because her marker stretched her leg as much as possible to avoid Lloyd receiving the ball. In her effort, the ball got deflected towards Heath's position. Lloyd, indeed, was part of the play.

We have reviewed three controversial cases, each with different signatures. In the first one, regarding Griezmann's penalty, there might be no foul, but it is difficult to claim with certainty that it was a wrong decision. In the second case, Iran´s penalty kick, the referee saw what (almost) no one else saw. It is challenging to jump without extending your arms, and it is practically impossible to do it at the highest level of competition in a World Cup. The referee, even after reviewing the VAR, felt that that was not the case and ruled a penalty kick. The third case is the opposite of the second case. It is true that maybe live Lloyd's position is difficult to check, but the video footage (including the one that the referee saw) clearly shows that the American forward had a saying in the action even if she did not touch the ball.

The theories of justice tend to search for a fair distribution of some given variable, be it income, wealth, or similar, under some specific precepts depending on its authors. In that sense, a just society requires a foundation, such as a social contract, which under Rawls' views, for instance, requires a veil of ignorance. It follows that any of the above controversial actions could all be just because under the existing social contract, the rules are well defined, and there is a consensus on implementation methods. The current social contract in soccer did not emerge from a veil of ignorance. Still, its historical roots have allowed it to evolve so that the resulting guidelines, the rules of the game, are unanimously accepted by the world of soccer.

---

[13] https://time.com/5613165/var-womens-world-cup-soccer/ visited May 13, 2021. https://www.nytimes.com/2019/06/20/sports/uswnt-sweden-score.html#link-303 0cf00 visited May 13, 2021.

However, unanimity must be interpreted with care. During the World Cup, every player, manager, fan, and reporter was aware of the rules of the game and willing to abide by them. In the long run, the story is different because there are, and have always been, voices that seek to improve, adjust, or modify the existing consensus. Calls for change are loud when the society is unjust as defined by some acceptable distribution of the relevant variable decisions in the case of soccer.

Thus, what we saw in the field during the World Cup, including the actions described above, as controversial as they might be, is a judge enforcing the unanimously accepted rules. In that sense, justice prevails because the referee is fully aware of the existing social contract and her obligation to distribute decisions abiding by the accepted guidelines during a soccer match. Still, although a consensus is not a necessary condition to achieve justice, injustice arises when a judge fails to use all the instruments at her disposal. But, when a referee interprets based on all the available information, the debate turns towards the fairness of the decision. Thus, to achieve fairness, first justice has to be met. Everything, however, depends on how to interpret the existing rules. In the latter lies the complexity of soccer.

Fairness is, thus, another matter. Assume that decisions are the key variable to distribute in a soccer match. Recall Chapter 2, where fairness, for some authors, was related to the distribution patterns that focus on the less fortunate. Such is not the case in soccer. Others defend that the existing distribution is fair if individuals are entitled to their holding. When limiting the analysis to a soccer match, as opposed to the broader exercise done in Chapter 2, it is difficult to follow this definition of fairness because the enforcer's decision is, in principle, independent of its history. Indeed, according to the psychological literature, individuals tend to be inconsistent over time (Kahneman et al., 2021). It is not uncommon for any person to change a decision when facing a similar event. Or, in soccer terms, a referee will not always be consistent in her decisions, thus questioning the validity of Nozick's fairness concept in soccer.

Fairness is a property of competition and of processes (Scanlon, 1977). It does not have to do with distributive justice but with how to enforce the just institutions that have emerged from the social contract.

The three examples considered all relate to the interpretation of the rules. Days, months, years after the game concluded, the debate on the validity of the decision is still afloat. All agents involved in the game have an opinion, some based on a detailed analysis of the event, others simply on a gut feeling. Concluding that the final call was wrong in Cedric's and Lloyds's case but probably correct in Griezmann's penalty is perhaps true in the first two cases but unclear in the latter. They would be just decisions if the referee used all the available information in each case. It is unfair if the decision is incorrect, even when the referees tried to be just.

Controversy-wise, life was simpler in the past when the referee decided, and there was little way of disputing it. At the 1954 final or the 1966 final, the linesman had just one chance to see the entire play. Numerous factors can explain, in retrospect, almost any mistake. They were running, their line of sight was not clear, or maybe their perspective was not adequate.

In the 1990 final (except for Calderon's foul), the entire world got to see several instant replays from different angles. Everyone, but the one that mattered, the referee. In 2018 and 2019, this is no longer true. The obvious advantage of the VAR technology is that now, for sure, the entire world gets to see the replay, including the referee. The referees now have a new instrument to impart justice, even if their final call is unfair.

VAR and Stoppage Time

A typical exercise in the literature is to check how VAR affects the playing time. Based on the data and procedures already discussed, the estimate of minutes devoted to VAR considers the precise minute (and second) since the event started until the referee's definitive ruling ordering the game to continue.

The stoppage time per VAR intervention was, on average, one minute and fifty-three seconds during the World Cup in France and one minute and twenty-eight seconds in Russia. However, the means are not statistically different. Figure 4.5 depicts the time devoted to VAR per cause.

In the female Word Cup, the most time devoted to VAR relates to goals and penalties awarded and penalties not awarded. In contrast, during the male World Cup, the leading causes were goals not awarded, card upgrades, and penalties awarded. Hardly any overlap between tournaments.

OPTA records referees' contentious decisions and a stoppage in play, such as a player injury. Figure 4.6 compares VAR interventions as defined above with OPTA's stoppage time from non-VAR-related events. In absolute figures, it is apparent that VAR adds stoppage time because not all contentious referee decisions before the use of the new technology implied extra time, particularly events such as card upgrades. Figure 4.6,

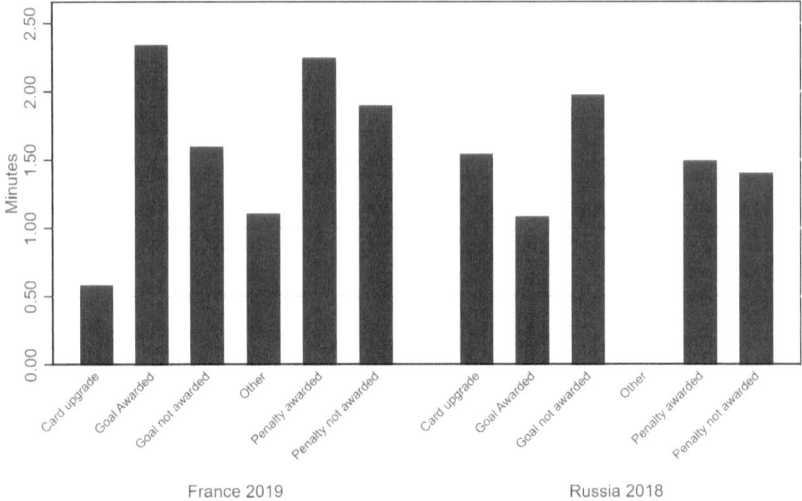

Fig. 4.5 Time used by VAR interventions causes (*Source* Opta. Own calculations)

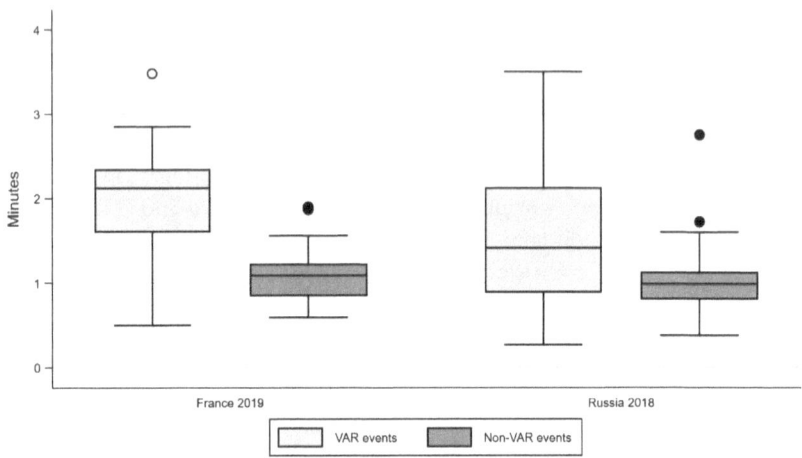

Fig. 4.6 Stoppage in per match average time per event (*Source* Opta. Own calculations)

depicting the average number of minutes devoted to either VAR o non-VAR events, reveals that VAR events take, individually, more time than other events.

Non-VAR events, with a tighter distribution than VAR events, tend to take less time, around a minute, especially in France 2019. VAR events are sparser, particularly in Russia 2018, supporting the hypothesis that given the novelty of the technology, the decisions lacked the necessary homogeneity. It might also be that controversy takes time, and by definition, VAR events are controversial.

Referees and VAR

All the paraphernalia around the VAR technology ultimately depends on the referee and her interpretation of the rules. Thus, it is worth reviewing if there is an obvious pattern in its use. Twenty-eight referees dealt with Russia's sixty-four games. Twenty-four in France's fifty-two games. The most prolific referee in the former was Néstor Pitana, the Argentinian, who handled five games, including the final. Three referees dealt with four games in France 2019, Edina Alves, Marie Beaudoin, and Stéphanie Frappart; the latter refereed the final match between the United States and the Netherlands.

Figure 4.7 depicts the number of VAR interventions per referee per game and the number of fouls. It might be that referees that tend to call more fouls are more prone to use the VAR technology. The number of observations is limited when focusing only on the World Cups, among other reasons, because seventeen referees officiated only one match and thirteen, two. Still, it is worth exploring a potential correlation that could suggest further inquiries.

Consistent with the ongoing discussion, there are more VAR interventions in France than in Russia, but no visible patterns arise. The men's World Cup had fewer VAR interventions per game than the women's, but there is no apparent connection with the number of fouls.

Figure 4.8 checks for a correlation between the stoppage time of a VAR intervention and OPTA's contentious decisions described earlier. Again, as before, there is little evidence of any correlation between referees that get involved in non-VAR controversial decisions with VAR stoppage times.

A common complaint in the history of the World Cups is that referees are biased for or against specific teams, in this case, certain countries.

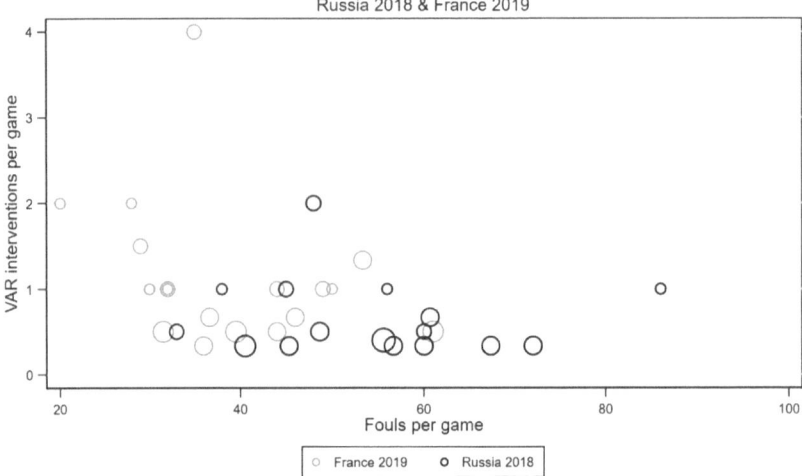

Fig. 4.7 VAR interventions and fouls per referee per game (*Note* The bubbles size is positively correlated to the number of games refereed. The graph consideres only referees that used VAR. *Source* Opta. Own calculations)

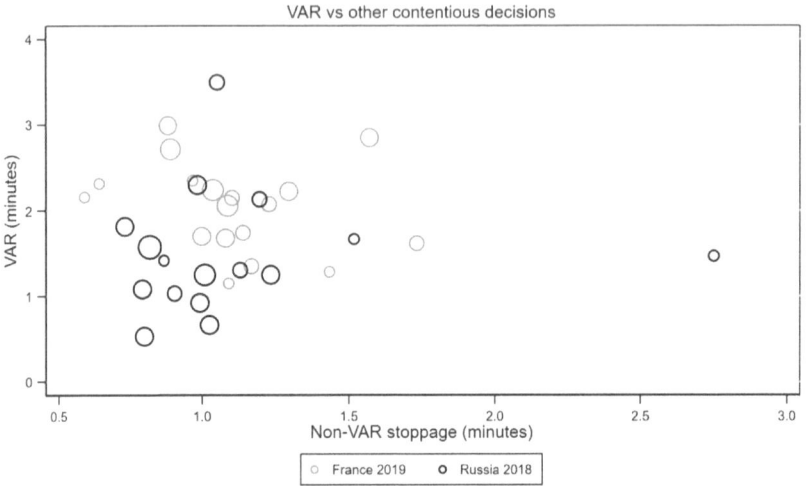

Fig. 4.8 Stoppage time per referee per game (*Note* The bubbles size is positively correlated to the number of games refereed. The graph consideres only referees that used VAR. *Source* Opta. Own calculations)

Unfortunately, few observations are available to determine such a hypothesis statistically, but it is possible to review and check qualitatively whether such a story might be true. Figure 4.9 depicts the number of for and against VAR interventions per team during Russia 2018. The figure is normalized by the number of games played to account for the number of games played.

On the "for" side, Spain and Portugal benefited more than the rest, although Portugal is also among the top four countries on the "against" side. It is difficult to establish criteria to determine what "too much" for or against decisions are. Given that it is the World Cup, the hypothesis is that VAR potentially favors top teams while referees adversely rule against historically weak teams.

Although Portugal and Spain are among the best teams globally, other obvious choices such as Germany or Brazil are not in the "for" ranking. Of particular relevance is Germany, a natural candidate for such favorable treatment because they were reigning World Champions and got knocked out in the first round for the first time since France 1938. Moreover, teams with little historical background in the World Cup, such as Saudi

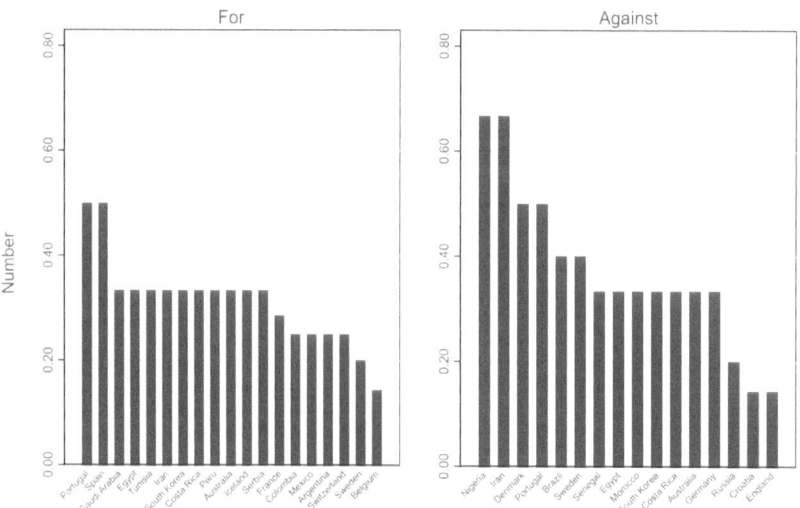

Fig. 4.9 Russia 2018 VAR decisions per game played (*Source* Opta. Own calculations)

Arabia, Egypt, Tunisia, and Iran, had relatively favorable VAR rulings. Although the top teams in the "against" ranking are Nigeria and Iran, not among the historical best, Brazil and Portugal are among the top five. Overall, there is no substantive indication suggesting that referees are systematically biased.

The France 2019 World Cup data portrayed in Fig. 4.10 initially suggests a different story than that observed in Russia 2018. The top four teams favored by VAR rulings, Brazil, Australia, England, and the United States, are among the world's top. VAR benefiting top teams the most is probably related to the significant quality differential between the top and average teams in women's soccer. However, France is by far the team most hurt by VAR rulings. Indeed, France is not historically the best team, but they were the World Cup host.

There is no conclusive evidence suggesting that referees were systematically biased during either the male or female World Cups. As noted elsewhere, reviewing each of the fifty-nine VAR interventions is futile and boring, but checking many of them suggests that no systematic mistakes

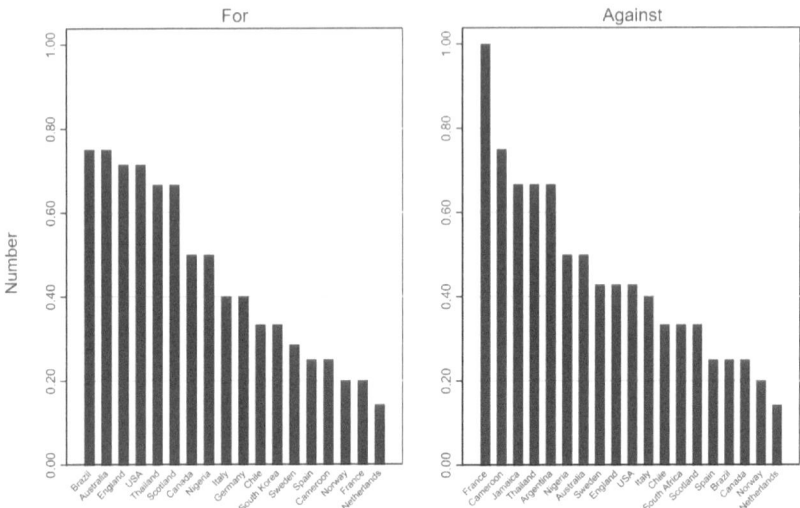

Fig. 4.10 France 2019 VAR decisions per game played (*Source* Opta. Own calculations)

favor top teams. In some cases, top teams seem to be treated favorably, but the result is the opposite on other occasions.

When VAR is Ignored

According to a defined set of situations, the VAR technology is open for the referee to use when necessary. However, on occasions, it is not used, even when it is apparent that it should. A referee who chooses not to use VAR is not only unfair but unjust.

An obvious example occurred during the second matchday for Group E in Russia 2018 when Switzerland defeated Serbia 2–1. Drawing 1–1, in the 65th minute, the Serbian Tadic crosses from the right towards the six-yard goal. Mitrovic attacks the ball, ready to strike for an almost guaranteed goal. As soon as the ball left Tadic's boot, two Swiss players, one from behind and the other in front, embraced Mitrovic, almost like a hug. He could not properly attack the ball, could not jump, and while falling (simultaneously with his two Swiss stamps), the ball gently hit his head. It was a foul for the spectators in the stadium; it was a penalty kick once checking the replay. Perhaps a casual observer could believe that the two Swiss players were simply hugging the Serbian and that it was not a foul but a signal of friendship. But the referee was not a casual observer. In either case, it is not easy to understand why the referee did not check the VAR. The referee could interpret the action in a specific way, but it is the type of play that might serve as an example of when to use VAR if one is unsure.

In the extra time of the round of sixteen match between Colombia and England in the Russian World Cup, another controversial decision lacked VAR participation when the ball went out in the English half. To resume the game, two balls were sent back to the field. One of the balls was kicked out by an English player, bouncing immediately back to the field. Pickford, the goalkeeper, kicks that ball away, prompting Young to resume play. However, Pickford's ball rebounded on the billboards, bouncing back into the pitch, provoking the referee to stop the game.

Pickford kicked that same ball away again, while an English field player passed the other ball back to Young. The referee whistled to play on; Young picked the ball and threw-in towards Maguire. Crucially, when he made the throw-in, there was only one football on the field. Meanwhile, the other ball, the one that Pickford had kicked out, bounced once again, and while Young was executing the throw-in to Maguire (following the play on order), he was looking at Pickford's ball. Having heard the whistle and seeing that Young had already put the ball into play, the linesman bent slightly and stopped the ball from returning back into the field with his right hand.

Meanwhile, Maguire was still looking at Pickford's ball, and because it was on a trajectory to return towards the pitch, he was walking towards it. He did not see Young's ball, which smoothly passed by him. Falcao, paying attention to the ball at play, run to it with Stones rushing desperately behind him, while Maguire anxiously raised his hand, asking the referee to stop the game. Seeing Maguire's reaction, the referee whistled as Falcao passed the ball to Bacca, who scored, although by then, the English defenders, having listened to the whistle, had already stopped pressing. The referee signaled the Colombian players that he had stopped the game because there were two balls inside the field. That is not true. The footage of the action clearly shows that only one ball was at play. The referee did not review the VAR.

The Colombian press wrote that the action was "disallowed with no apparent reason" because "the linesman never allowed a second ball to enter."[14] The English media essentially, on their part, ignored the event, focusing instead on the VAR not assisting the referee when the Colombian midfielder, Barrios, appeared to deliberately headbutt Henderson's chest during the game's first half. There was "not much for in the gesture," wrote the English press, but "technically it was a red card."[15] The game footage shows the referee touching his ear, apparently speaking to the fourth official, before given Barrios a yellow card.[16]

The most notorious non-VAR interventions probably occurred in the game between England and Cameroon in the round of sixteen match in France 2019. The Africans took a very rough approach and, although there were four VAR interventions in the game, the figure might be short. Maybe, who knows, recalling Pele´s elbow described in the introduction,

---

[14] https://www.eltiempo.com/mundial-rusia-2018/era-o-no-gol-de-bacca-el-arbitro-jose-borda-responde-239102 visited May 13, 2020.

[15] https://www.theguardian.com/football/live/2018/jul/03/world-cup-2018-colombia-v-england-buildup-live?page=with:block-5b3bc83ae4b074b33454fb49#liveblog-navigation visited May 13, 2020.

[16] https://www.independent.co.uk/sport/football/world-cup/england-vs-colombia-referee-world-cup-2018-mark-geiger-penalty-red-card-raheem-sterling-video-watch-highlights-a8429826.html visited May 12, 2020.

Yvonne Leuko stuck her right elbow straight into England's Nikita Parris' jaw. The main difference with Pele's play, beyond the fact that her abilities are far away from the King's, was that the English player was attacking, while Pele, one could argue, was anticipating a tackle. The Cameroonian was defending, and her action against Parris was aggression in its simplest form. The referee saw the elbow, gave Leuko a yellow card, but refrained from using VAR to assess the need to upgrade the card to red.

Later on, in that same game, Leuko decided to emulate Franz Rijkaard's spit on Völler's hair in the 1990 World Cup. Upon being sent off, Rijkaard runs towards the German from behind and spits to his hair. Völler got a yellow card because he faced up to Rijkaard, who later apologized, explaining that he had simply lost his head. I am not aware of Leuko apologizing for spitting from behind Duggan's stretched arm. The English player showed the referee the white spittle dripping down but, still, she did not request the VAR.

VAR was not used publicly in these events, but it may be that some communication did exist between the referee and the VAR room. However, currently, the referee is the ultimate decision-maker, and it is them who chose not to use it.

References

Caruso, E. M., Burns, Z. C., & Converse, B. A. (2016). Slow motion increases perceived intent. *Proceedings of the National Academy of Sciences, 113*(33), 9250–9255.

Kahneman, D., Siboni, O., and Sunstein, C. (2021). *Noise. A flaw in human judgement*. Little Brown Spark.

Kubayi, A., Larkin, P., & Toriola, A. (2021). The impact of video assistant referee (VAR) on match performance variables at men's FIFA World Cup tournaments. *Proceedings of the Institution of Mechanical Engineers, Part P: Journal of Sports Engineering and Technology*, 1754337121997581.

Scanlon, T. M. (1977). Rights, goals, and fairness. *Erkenntnis, 11*(1), 81–95.

Sperl, L., Hüttner, N., & Schroeger, A. (2021). Why Do Actions in Slow Motion Appear to Last Longer? On the Effect of Video Speed Information. *Perception, 50*(1), 69–79.

Spitz, J., Moors, P., Wagemans, J., & Helsen, W. F. (2018). The impact of video speed on the decision-making process of sports officials. *Cognitive Research: Principles and Implications, 3*(1), 1–10.

Spitz, J., Wagemans, J., Memmert, D., Williams, A. M., & Helsen, W. F. (2021). Video assistant referees (VAR): The impact of technology on decision making in association football referees. *Journal of Sports Sciences, 39*(2), 147–153.

CHAPTER 5

Why and How to Improve VAR

Abstract This chapter debates about the use of VAR, drawing from the discussion in previous chapters. It shows, using several cases, that although the quest for justice and fairness is a natural objective in any society, fully achieving it is not possible. Although VAR was a relative success in Russia 2018 and France 2019, its use should be adjusted because it is extracting a toll in soccer: the sport relies on its dynamics for survival. The objective should not be to minimize errors but, instead, to make justice, maximizing fairness.

Keyword Fairness · Justice · Social Contract · VAR adjustment · Mistakes · Controversy

The quest for universal fairness under a just environment is the quest for the holy grail. It might be there, but the evidence suggests that, at least, it is very difficult to find. The history of the rules of soccer is the history of the quest for an equitable society, one where the rules should lead to a just world. In that sense, the process of designing a set of institutions that leads to a theoretically just society has been a success.

© The Author(s), under exclusive license to Springer Nature
Switzerland AG 2021
J. Tovar, *On Fairness, Justice, and VAR*,
Palgrave Pivots in Sports Economics,
https://doi.org/10.1007/978-3-030-84814-9_5

The existing social contract has evolved since the dawn of soccer. In its origin, a homogenous group of people designed a set of guidelines in, arguably, a similar fashion to what some political philosophers had imagined for their ideal society. However, as society evolved, so did soccer and its little round world. The idea of a social contract derived from other models, maybe stemming from the concept of validating one's acts with others, remains.

In that sense, soccer tends to be a just society because the referees are inclined to abide by the universally accepted rules. The distribution of rulings is potentially unbiased. When interpretation emerges, fairness (or unfairness) arises. However, the rules are not always followed, even with a set of widely accepted guidelines. On occasions, maybe in good faith, maybe because of negligence, or perhaps because they have chosen not to follow the rules, the referees make unjust calls, implying an unfair outcome. Overall, VAR is a step further in seeking justice because it slows the game to allow the judge to review in detail a given controversial event.

The case of the Serbian Mitrovic described above is not novel in the history of the World Cup. In a way, it is similar to what happened in one of the greatest matches in history. Italy faced Brazil in the second-round game during the World Cup held in Spain in 1982. For a generation of Latin-Americans, not old enough to have seen Pele's Brazil, that Brazilian team remains the most exuberant example of attacking football with an unparalleled sense of elegance and grace.

Brazil only needed to draw that game to play the semifinals. Italy, also full of stars, backed by a strong defense and a striker in which until that day only Bearzot, the manager, believed in, needed to win. After 40 min, Paolo Rossi had scored twice for Italy while Socrates, following a magic pass between lines by Zico, had briefly drawn the game. With five minutes to go in the first half, Socrates passed to Zico surrounded by Italian defenders, just a couple of yards inside the box. Man-marked by Gentile, famous for annulling the greatest opposition stars including Maradona in the previous game, Zico runs parallel to the goal line trying to protect the ball while controlling it. Surprised by that movement, Gentile stretched his right arm to grab Zico. Instead, he snatched and tore the yellow Brazilian shirt while Zico, falling, could not shoot properly. Given the obviousness of Gentile's action, Falcao, Toninho Cerezo, and Leandro all raised their hands, expecting a penalty kick. At the same time, Zico got up, showing the referee the giant hole of his torn and now worthless shirt.

Unexpectedly, the referee called an offside, impossible because when Socrates was passing, Gentile was behind Zico, and Bergomi was at least a foot closer to its goal line than the two main characters of this event. In short, Gentile pulled Zico's shirt so hard that he tore it, threw the Brazilian to the ground, and the referee decided against the evident penalty kick. With no VAR to check, unlike in Mitrovic's move against Switzerland thirty-six years later, the decision was the same; no penalty ruled in either case.

Later that game, following Rossi's hattrick, Antognoni scored a fourth goal for Italy in a counterattack, making it impossible for Brazil to equalize in the approximately four minutes remaining. The video footage shows Paolo Rossi a couple of yards inside the box, passing the ball back to Orialli, who crosses the ball from right to left past two Brazilian defenders. Antognoni arrives at the precise instant ready to score the goal within the six-yard line. When Orialli passes the ball, the defender is stepping on the six-yard line, while Antognoni, at the other end of that box, is one yard early of the line. It was Italy's fourth, no offside.

Once again, with no VAR to check, the referee's decision stood. Once again, the VAR technology is no guarantee that the referee would have taken the correct decision as Heath's shot in the game between the United States and Sweden in 2019 proofs. But, VAR technology is a helpful instrument in many, if not most, circumstances.

However, no matter the rules or the faith put on the mechanism, it is still heavily dependent on interpretation. It makes little sense to evaluate VAR based on actions where a set of professional referees have a unanimous opinion. The objective of the VAR technology, beyond confirming the obvious, is to improve the decisions when the event is unclear. In other words, to make the game fairer considering that soccer is always opened to the unexpected.

Indeed, in Brazil's opening match in Argentina in 1978, the unexpected happened. In the last minute of the game against Sweden, the South Americans earned a corner kick. At precisely minute 45 of the second half Nelinho prepares the ball. He strikes it at minute 45 and six seconds. Approximately two seconds later, Zico heads the ball from inside the six-yard box scoring the winner. However, with the ball in the air, Clive Thomas, the Welsh referee, decided that the game was over, depriving Brazil of the victory. The referee, one might imagine, was unaware of the 1891's match between Stoke City and Aston Villa that originated injury time. Similar to what happened with Bacca in Russia

2018, it was technically never a goal because the referee blew the whistle before the actual shot. In both cases, the referee made a controversial, if not wrong, decision that was impossible to fix by VAR's current rules of engagement. The shot for goal was never valid because the ball was not at play.

The above situations suggest that yesterday as today, soccer has some injustice embedded in it. Zico's header made worldwide headlines, with networks extensively repeating the corner kick across the globe. Bacca's shot, however, hardly made the news beyond South America, among other reasons, because the live broadcast did not repeat it. In general, referees tend to distribute decisions justly, following the widely known guidelines, but they make mistakes. Unfair decisions are on occasions shared by the entire planet, sometimes by a small group. Zico's header amazed the whole soccer community. Bacca's shot frustrated only Colombians. Croatians were also frustrated after a VAR intervention during the final game of the 2018 World Cup.

With a draw on the scoreboard, a corner kick for France ended up with the ball on the penalty spot. The rules of the game for the World Cup stated that to consider a handball, the referee should consider the movement of the hands towards the ball and the distance of the opponent from the ball. It also stated that the hand's position did not necessarily imply an offense.

Griezmann took the corner kick from the right towards the near post. France's Matuidi rushed for the ball in front of Perisic inside the six-yard box. They jumped simultaneously for the ball, Matuidi missed it, ultimately hitting Perisic's hand. The video footage shows that both players raise their hands at the same time when jumping and simultaneously lower them when going down. It is then, when Matuidi missed, with Perisic's arm falling, mimicking the French player's arms, that the ball hit the Croatian's left hand.

There is no doubt that the ball hit his hand, which was coming down very close to his waist. It took the referee over two minutes to turn around and rule a penalty kick. The Argentinian press backed the Argentinian referee saying that Perisic's "slight wrist movement" was determinant.[1] El País, the Spanish newspaper, wrote that "by chance, the

---

[1] https://www.nacion.com/puro-deporte/futbol-internacional/analistas-arbitrales-fue-correcta-la-decision-de/57FUUE2T3JG6PE5YVRUAI2MAKY/story/ visited May 26 2021.

ball hit Perisic's left arm."[2] Considering the difficulty to consciously move the hand slightly in the air without knowing that the adversary would miss it, the decision was, to say the least, a highly controversial decision. Bordering injustice, the referee's decision was probably unfair. As it has happened so many times in history, it all boils down to how to interpret the rules.

Having reviewed VAR, from a certain point of view, validates Pitana's decision. Not like what had happened in France's first goal. As England's claim that the German's equalizer during the 1966 final match originated in a nonexistent foul, such happened in the 2018 final. Griezmann received the ball, his back to the goal, slightly skewed to the right, about 25 yards from Croatia's goal line. In one swift movement, he turned around only to be tackled down by Brozović, or so decided the referee.

The slow-motion is crystal clear. Upon turning 180 degrees, Griezmann sees the Croatian coming, gently pushes the ball forward and dives. Brozović, even if it was his intention, did not have a chance to tackle the French. When he arrived, Griezmann was already falling, and, if anything, he moves his left leg to guarantee some contact with the defender. VAR did not have the power to interfere in this event, among other reasons, because the foul was outside the box.

Nevertheless, one can assume that the VAR room did notice the nonexisting foul. Marca, the Spanish sports newspaper, wrote that Griezmann "dived to the grass when he saw Marcelo Brozović nearby. Nestor Pitana called it on what was already universal news, a Frenchman cheating on an Argentine."[3] The Spanish newspaper La Vanguardia wrote that the goal came "after a non-existent foul on Griezmann."[4] It was not a foul, but once the referee whistled, there was no turning back.

Griezmann's free kick ended in Mandzukić's own goal. In trying to avoid the ball reaching Pogba's head, Mandzukić stretched his body as much as possible, unlucky enough to score France's opener. The

---

[2] https://elpais.com/deportes/2018/07/15/mundial_futbol/1531664926_029675. html May 26, 2021.

[3] https://www.marca.com/claro-mx/futbol/mundial/2018/07/15/5b4b7b37268e 3e706c8b45c0.html June 1, 2021.

[4] https://www.lavanguardia.com/deportes/mundial-2018-rusia/20180715/459216 34518/var-final-mundial-rusia-francia-croacia-griezmann-perisic-penalti.html   June   6, 2021.

linesman never raised the flag, and VAR did not intervene, but the repetition, although not from the best angle, suggests that Pogba might have been offside when Griezmann kicked the ball. It was a goal; it was the World Cup final; VAR had not been used yet in the game; the available technology should have been used.

Justice is not met when the judge does not use all the tools at her disposal to make a fair decision. In this case, the referee decided not to use VAR. Sports Illustrated asked the same question: "Croatia will ask, quite reasonably, why Pitana did not consult VAR over France's first goal in which Paul Pogba, who was interfering with play to the extent that he was actually touching Mario Mandzukic as he flicked Antoine Griezmann's free kick into his own net, was offside as the ball was delivered."[5]

For justice to prevail, the arbitrator needs to understand the guidelines she is expected to follow while using all the tools at her disposal to deliver a fair decision. When the referee refused to check VAR for a potential offside, a decision well within the rules of the game, he denied justice to a team. The referee went against the prevailing social contract, and an unfair decision stood.

The Croatians, it turns out, found no justice whether the referee followed the rules or whether he did not. The conclusion is straightforward. No social contract, not even in the world of soccer, is perfect. Achieving perfection is probably a chimera. Although ending injustice is a desirable end, it is in this context that lies much of the debate on the theories of justice. Thinkers from different roots and with different approaches question permanently what the best route is to achieving an equalitarian (in some sense discussed in Chapter 2) society.

Arguably, any society has been continuously debating for centuries what the best path is. Soccer, as an integral part of the community since its foundation, is no different. It has been seeking its own approach to justice for over a century, building along the way the institutions that rule the game.

The final game of the 2018 World Cup is an excellent example of the complexity of such a quest. But it also demonstrates the need to keep pushing ahead. Not only may the judge set aside the existing rules, but, moreover, the social contract might be incomplete. True, the debate on France's first goal has not gained the historical proportion that England's

---

[5] https://www.si.com/soccer/2018/07/15/france-world-cup-final-var-referee-contro versy-perisic-griezmann-croatia visited May 30, 2021.

1966 third goal ruling has, or even the 1990 penalty and no penalties decisions. But a 1960s controversy replicated in 2018 when the technology exists to avoid such potential mistakes. The adjustment to the rules and their interpretation is a constant in soccer. That is, the social contract needs to evolve permanently.

VAR has failed to achieve complete justice. But that was not the intention of the new technology. It was simply an adjustment to the prevailing social contract. So is VAR an advance or a setback?

The climax of this game is the goal. No Italian, even those unborn in 1982, will ever forget Tardelli's fists and head shaking side to side while screaming with exhilaration his goal in the World Cup Final against Germany. Fabio Grosso is an example of this. In 2006, he scored the winner in the semifinal against Germany. When Tardelli scored that goal in the Bernabeu Stadium, Grosso was four, but his celebration paid a clear tribute to Italy's 1982s goal celebration.

Not only Italians have such climatic celebrations. Colombians will forever remember Freddy Rincón's last-minute equalizer celebration against Germany in 1990. Brazilians have embedded Bebeto's 1994 celebration in their mind who, joined by Romario and Mazinho, rocked his arms in homage to his son, born a couple of days earlier. Spaniards will forever recall Iniesta's 2010 winner goal celebration when he removed his jersey to display an inscription in his undershirt to honor his buddy dead a year earlier. "It is hard to describe the impact of [Zimmermann's] broadcast to non-Germans, let alone transport its content into another language," wrote Hesse (2003) on the reporter's celebration of Germany's third goal in 1954. Resembling "one of his South American colleagues, who had long since taken up the habit of going nuts when covering football," Zimmerman, the reporter in charge of communicating what was happening in Bern to Germany, shouted "Rahn schiesst … Tor! Tor! Tor! Tor!", that is, "Rahn shoots, … Goal! Goal! Goal! Goal!" Hesse (2003).

Now, imagine that VAR cut off the celebration of any of these goals. Imagine that Tardelli's run was cut short, that Romario and Mazinho had no time to rock their arms with Bebeto, that Iniesta had to put his jersey back on, or that after Zimmerman's first Tor, everyone had to wait for one, two, three, or four minutes until the referee approved the goal.

There are many reasons for soccer's prevalence for over a century. A non-negligible one is the legend built behind many of those celebrations. Italians celebrate the 1982 World Cup in Spain, but it is the picture of

Tardelli's goal that gives goosebumps. VAR, indeed, does extract a toll on soccer. From a certain point of view, it is not difficult to understand those who claim that the VAR has dwindled the game's essence.

Unlike in baseball, basketball, or American football, goals in soccer are a rarity. Even so, the VAR has proven in Russia and France to be an advancement that, looking back in history, has the potential to avoid many unfair decisions. Still, it needs adjustments, particularly in two distinct facets: the events to be reviewed and the referees.

A premise to keep in mind is that soccer was born, evolved, and survived as the most successful sport in history without VAR technology. Thus, despite the good intentions, too much VAR might not have the desired positive effects. The numerous accounts of events that used or should have used VAR allow for a detailed review of when its use might be optimal.

Soccer is a dynamic game, impossible, even with VAR, to have both teams feel permanently and simultaneously treated fairly. In line with this reality, the objective of the instrument should not be to minimize errors but, instead, to deal with obvious mistakes. In other words, it should aim to make justice, maximizing fairness.

No VAR technology would ever agree on whether Germany's penalty in the 1990 final against Argentina was indeed a foul or not. Decades later, many still find an edge to conclude in either direction. Moreover, such events enrich the history of the World Cups. The VAR must retain the game dynamics, even if it cannot deal with every contentious decision. The technology, widely discussed, is unable to deal with every event uncontroversially. Beyond the decisions made, the objective is to use VAR without having the show of the referee going to a television screen. It is not a matter of the time wasted, relevant, but not determinant; it is a matter, let me be repetitive, of keeping the game's dynamics.

To achieve this objective, the game must have two referees with the power invested in making decisions about the match. An on-field referee would operate as it has since the dawn of time. An off-field referee will decide whether the event is sufficiently interpretable to make the use of VAR worth it.

Consider a frequent event, fouls, for instance. When a referee whistles a foul anywhere on the pitch, the VAR room must have the authority to decide whether the referee made a mistake or not. If a player dives, she must also receive a yellow card. The strategy implies transferring more power to the VAR room, as it would ultimately decide if a foul already called by the referee was, in fact, worth the whistle. If the VAR room requires too much time, then the event is not uncontroversial, and it is best to move on with the game. Maybe penalty kicks, because of their significance in the game, deserve a second look. This would minimize having the referee going to the VAR area to check a television set while a billion people are looking at her. It is not only the time wasted. It is reducing the pressure on a human being.

Thus, a foul like Griezmann's fall in the game against Australia in Russia in 2018 would have no VAR intervention because what happened is opened to debate. On the contrary, a foul like that on Calderon in the 1990 final game would not be unchecked had it been called. It was an apparent foul. The strategy is to optimize the use of the technology to make the game fairer, wherever is possible to make it fairer, but acknowledging that achieving complete consensus is an impossible mission.

The VAR (room) would enforce offsides when the pass finishes in a goal or any other event that favors the potential offender. Thus, the role of the linesman, offside-wise, changes to calling obvious offsides where the game must be stopped. Events like those of Puskas third in 1954 or France's first goal in 2018 would not be controversial thanks to the dozens of cameras available in a World Cup. Moreover, having the VAR room check the potential event in real-time would not cut those goal celebrations that are unique to soccer.

The entire show, of course, depends on the referees' understanding and following the widely accepted rules of the game. A referee should not end the game while the ball is in the air in a corner kick or only one ball in the field, claiming otherwise. In the South American qualifiers for Qatar 2022, a Colombian referee was banned by Conmebol, the South American ruling body, because he denied Uruguay a goal even after reviewing VAR. He saw an offside where no one else saw it. No one saw it because it was not offside. Similarly, in the opening match of the 2020 UEFA Euro game between Italy and Turkey (held in 2021 due to the pandemic), the Dutch linesman flagged offside in a corner kick. There are no offsides in the first pass of a corner kick. Thus, the level of an off-field referee should match that of an on-field referee with both perfectly aware of the existing rules.

Injustice, unavoidable as it is, will still exist because referees will always make mistakes. However, having a VAR referee making the calls reduces direct pressure on the on-field referee while keeping the game alive, reducing the stoppage time cause by using the technology. The stoppage time indeed tends to be recovered with injury time, but it is also true that the VAR events take more time than non-VAR contentious events.

Using VAR in subjectively, non-contentious events allows for correcting some of the unavoidable human aspects. For example, there is strong evidence that slow-motion has an impact on the decision made. Pending some experimentation in soccer, the off-field referee can have the support that has shown some positive results in the experimental literature, such as revealing the speed of the video footage. The approach can also correct other existing but less known biases. Kranjec et al. (2010), for instance, show that two referees watching the same play from different angles are predisposed to make different calls on whether it is or is not a foul. The VAR non-field referee, having access from various perspectives, will have a lower propensity to bias.

Still, referees make mistakes, and their decisions remain controversial because of what Kahneman et al. (2021) call noise, thus leading to the claim that unfairness is inevitable.[6] Therefore, the objective is to design a VAR mechanism that reduces the well-known propensity of referees, as human beings, to judge wrongly.

There will always be contentious events because it is in the nature of soccer. The soccer community should openly assume that these events are part of what makes this sport unique. Pushing VAR forward in a direction that seeks to erase all controversy is a mistake. Such a path would attack the essence of the sport, that which allows for crazy celebrations. The VAR is a valuable and necessary instrument in modern soccer. But even the most advanced artificial intelligence algorithm will be unable to completely erase the discussions on the validity of some of its decisions. Out of 169 goals scored in Russia 2018, 16.6% were a penalty kick. That more than doubles the percentage of Brazil in 2014, just 7.6%, and it is substantially above the 10.3% of South Africa 2010. Controversy exists in every World Cup, VAR or no VAR. The proposal is to use the technology to deal with unfairness but keep the sport open to interpretation.

---

[6] Kahneman et al. (2021) p. 87.

References

Hesse, U. (2003). *Tor!: the story of German football*. WSC Books Limited.

Kranjec, A., Lehet, M., Bromberger, B., & Chatterjee, A. (2010). A sinister bias for calling fouls in soccer. *PloS one*, 5(7), e11667.

Kahneman, D., Siboni, O., and Sunstein, C. (2021). *Noise. A flaw in human judgement*. Little Brown Spark.

CHAPTER 6

Conclusion

Abstract This chapter draws together the main arguments and results. There is a relative consensus that injustice exists in society. Soccer, an integral part of society, also survives with some level of injustice embedded in it. Accepting that a controversy-free sport is unachievable implies that the VAR instrument should be adjusted. Design to help referees within specific parameters to avoid mistakes has achieved relative success. However, controversy remains because VAR cannot guarantee an improvement in every possible event. Acknowledging this while retaining soccer's dynamics will improve its little round world.

Keyword Video Assistant Referee · Justice · Fairness · Soccer · FIFA · Controversy

The VAR is the most significant application of technology within the game of soccer since its foundation in 1863. The debate on its effect has confronted two distinct opinions. On the one hand, some defend that the VAR is an affront against the core meaning of soccer. On the other hand, some understand that soccer needs to adapt itself to the reality of the twenty-first century. The truth probably lies somewhere in between.

© The Author(s), under exclusive license to Springer Nature
Switzerland AG 2021
J. Tovar, *On Fairness, Justice, and VAR*,
Palgrave Pivots in Sports Economics,
https://doi.org/10.1007/978-3-030-84814-9_6

Some of the world's most smart thinkers have been debating for a long time how to attain justice in the most equitably way possible. There is no conclusion. From Rawls's veil of ignorance, one understands that a major obstacle to achieving justice lies in the very nature of the human being. Indeed, in almost every theory of justice, the debate lies in how to overcome the intrinsic complications of dealing with the individual's preferences, almost by nature polluted by their perception of the world. The social contract proposal may stem from a world where no one is aware of where they stand or where they seek social support. In any case, the objective is to design guidelines that allow society to improve its well-being.

Soccer has the advantage that the guidelines, the rules of the game, have been accepted almost unanimously since its birth. In the beginning, the laws designed by a small homogenous group of individuals were enough to promote the game's expansion. Practitioners in England, Europe, or the World embraced the game and accepted its rules. When they did not, a different sport arose, from rugby to various versions of football in Australia or the United States. Central to our story, soccer, within its little round society, managed to design a set of institutions that had enough strength to disseminate the rules with enough credibility worldwide.

The soccer community constantly pushed for small or large twists in the game's rules keeping the sport alive. Although with a continuous debate, the current guidelines in any time of history were always unanimously known and accepted. As in many other facets of society, soccer required a judge, a referee to guarantee that the rules are appropriately applied. But referees are humans and prone to mistakes for many reasons.

The use of machines to help referees is relatively new in soccer. The debate should lie on the scope of the VAR. The idea of minimizing errors is noble and can make sense when analyzing past mistakes. However, that objective may find itself crashing against reality. Is it possible to achieve a state where controversial decisions disappear or, at the very least, where they but a few?

The answer is no. VAR is undoubtedly an improvement, but when used, it does not generate full uncontroversial decisions. Moreover, it has spawned another set of controversies that did not exist in the past. Why is VAR not used in certain situations? The numbers suggest that, overall, VAR in Russia 2018 and France 2019 was a success. It did prove that the mechanism has many positive things to offer football. However, the number of controversies is large enough to think about its use and how to operate the instrument better.

The path followed by VAR suggests that it seeks to reduce controversies even in situations in which it is not possible. It is imperative that soccer understands that justice is a desirable goal, but it is not necessarily achievable. Moreover, a n increase in the number of controversial decisions with VAR involved will, in time, impact its credibility.

This book concludes that an ideal approach is to optimize the decision in non-controversial events. Historically, there have been many mistakes in a variety of events that, with better video footage, would be a simple, non-controversial event. For example, consider Hurst's underside goal in 1966 or Zico's penalty kick in the game against Italy in 1982. A simple look at the screen would have denied England's goal and ruled a penalty kick for Brazil. Such should be VAR's objective.

On the contrary, it makes little sense to use VAR to decide, in slow-motion, whether a player in the air moved his hand on purpose or not to touch the ball. Soccer must retain its dynamics; it is in part what has propelled the sport to its special status worldwide.

To take absolute power from the main referee, FIFA and IFAB would need to review hundreds, if not thousands, of events within the last few years, both with and without VAR intervention. It is easy to talk about objective and subjective events but not easy to classify them, less in real-time. Thus, even after a thorough review of situations, there will be controversies. However, (near) obvious events will be controversy-free, and the game, in that sense, will be fairer.

On Pele's elbow on Fontes's face, the referee was right calling a foul for Brazil. A VAR review, as proposed here, would have expelled both players. The King's divine ball touch cannot be an excuse to remove the defender's teeth. Perfect justice is not achievable, but an improvement is always possible.

ANNEX

VAR interventions in Russia 2018 and France 2019

Word Cup	Team 1	Team 2	Period	Reason for VAR	Decision	VAR Outcome	Team favored by VAR
Russia 2018	Portugal	Spain	First Half	Goal Awarded	Confirmed	Goal	Spain
Russia 2018	France	Australia	Second Half	Penalty not awarded	Cancelled	Penalty	France
Russia 2018	Peru	Denmark	First Half	Penalty not awarded	Cancelled	Penalty	Peru
Russia 2018	Costa Rica	Serbia	Second Half	Card upgrade	Cancelled	Yellow Card	Serbia
Russia 2018	Sweden	Korea Republic	Second Half	Penalty not awarded	Cancelled	Penalty	Sweden
Russia 2018	Tunisia	England	First Half	Penalty awarded	Confirmed	Penalty	Tunisia
Russia 2018	Russia	Egypt	Second Half	Penalty not awarded	Cancelled	Penalty	Egypt
Russia 2018	Denmark	Australia	First Half	Penalty not awarded	Cancelled	Penalty	Australia
Russia 2018	Brazil	Costa Rica	Second Half	Penalty awarded	Cancelled	No Penalty	Costa Rica
Russia 2018	Nigeria	Iceland	Second Half	Penalty not awarded	Cancelled	Penalty	Iceland
Russia 2018	Saudi Arabia	Egypt	First Half	Penalty awarded	Confirmed	Penalty	Saudi Arabia
Russia 2018	Spain	Morocco	Second Half	Goal not awarded	Cancelled	Goal	Spain
Russia 2018	Iran	Portugal	Second Half	Penalty not awarded	Cancelled	Penalty	Portugal
Russia 2018	Iran	Portugal	Second Half	Card upgrade	Cancelled	Yellow Card	Portugal
Russia 2018	Iran	Portugal	Second Half	Penalty not awarded	Cancelled	Penalty	Iran
Russia 2018	Nigeria	Argentina	Second Half	Penalty not awarded	Confirmed	No Penalty	Argentina
Russia 2018	Mexico	Sweden	First Half	Penalty not awarded	Confirmed	No Penalty	Mexico
Russia 2018	Korea Republic	Germany	Second Half	Goal not awarded	Cancelled	Goal	South Korea
Russia 2018	Senegal	Colombia	First Half	Penalty awarded	Cancelled	No Penalty	Colombia
Russia 2018	Sweden	Switzerland	Second Half	Penalty awarded	Cancelled	No Penalty	Switzerland
Russia 2018	Brazil	Belgium	Second Half	Penalty not awarded	Confirmed	No Penalty	Belgium
Russia 2018	France	Croatia	First Half	Penalty not awarded	Cancelled	Penalty	France

(continued)

J. Tovar, *On Fairness, Justice, and VAR*,
Palgrave Pivots in Sports Economics,
https://doi.org/10.1007/978-3-030-84814-9

(continued)

France 2019	France	Korea Republic	First Half	Goal Awarded	Cancelled	No Goal	South Korea
France 2019	Spain	South Africa	Second Half	Penalty not awarded	Cancelled	Penalty	Spain
France 2019	Australia	Italy	First Half	Goal not awarded	Confirmed	No Goal	Australia
France 2019	Australia	Italy	Second Half	Penalty not awarded	Confirmed	No Penalty	Australia
France 2019	England	Scotland	First Half	Penalty not awarded	Cancelled	Penalty	England
France 2019	USA	Thailand	First Half	Penalty not awarded	Confirmed	No Penalty	Thailand
France 2019	USA	Thailand	First Half	Penalty not awarded	Confirmed	No Penalty	Thailand
France 2019	France	Norway	Second Half	Penalty not awarded	Cancelled	Penalty	France
France 2019	Australia	Brazil	First Half	Penalty not awarded	Confirmed	No Penalty	Brazil
France 2019	Australia	Brazil	Second Half	Goal not awarded	Cancelled	Goal	Australia
France 2019	Jamaica	Italy	First Half	Penalty not awarded	Cancelled	Penalty	Italy
France 2019	Jamaica	Italy	First Half	Other	Cancelled	Other-Cancelled	Italy
France 2019	Sweden	Thailand	Second Half	Penalty not awarded	Cancelled	Penalty	Sweden
France 2019	USA	Chile	Second Half	Penalty not awarded	Cancelled	Penalty	USA
France 2019	Nigeria	France	Second Half	Penalty not awarded	Cancelled	Penalty	Nigeria
France 2019	Nigeria	France	Second Half	Other	Cancelled	Other-Cancelled	Nigeria
France 2019	Scotland	Argentina	Second Half	Penalty not awarded	Cancelled	Penalty	Scotland
France 2019	Scotland	Argentina	Second Half	Other	Cancelled	Other-Cancelled	Scotland
France 2019	Netherlands	Canada	First Half	Penalty awarded	Cancelled	No Penalty	Netherlands
France 2019	Sweden	USA	Second Half	Goal Awarded	Confirmed	Goal	USA
France 2019	Thailand	Chile	Second Half	Penalty not awarded	Cancelled	Penalty	Chile
France 2019	Germany	Nigeria	First Half	Goal Awarded	Confirmed	Goal	Germany
France 2019	Germany	Nigeria	First Half	Penalty not awarded	Cancelled	Penalty	Germany
France 2019	Norway	Australia	First Half	Penalty awarded	Cancelled	No Penalty	Norway
France 2019	England	Cameroon	First Half	Goal not awarded	Cancelled	Goal	England
France 2019	England	Cameroon	Second Half	Goal Awarded	Cancelled	No Goal	England
France 2019	England	Cameroon	Second Half	Penalty not awarded	Confirmed	No Penalty	England
France 2019	England	Cameroon	Second Half	Card upgrade	Cancelled	Yellow Card	Cameroon
France 2019	France	Brazil	First Half	Goal Awarded	Cancelled	No Goal	Brazil
France 2019	France	Brazil	Second Half	Goal not awarded	Cancelled	Goal	Brazil
France 2019	Spain	USA	Second Half	Penalty not awarded	Confirmed	Penalty	USA
France 2019	Sweden	Canada	Second Half	Penalty not awarded	Cancelled	Penalty	Canada
France 2019	Sweden	Canada	Second Half	Penalty awarded	Cancelled	No Penalty	Canada
France 2019	England	USA	Second Half	Goal Awarded	Cancelled	No Goal	USA
France 2019	England	USA	Second Half	Penalty not awarded	Cancelled	Penalty	England
France 2019	England	Sweden	First Half	Goal Awarded	Cancelled	No Goal	Sweden
France 2019	USA	Netherlands	Second Half	Penalty not awarded	Cancelled	Penalty	USA

REFERENCES

Allingham, M. (2014). *Distributive justice*. Routledge.

Barry, B. (1989). *Theories of justice*. University of California Press.

Binmore, K. (2009). *Fairness as a natural phenomenon*. http://else.econ.ucl.ac.uk/papers/uploaded/332.pdf. Accessed March 31, 2021.

Bryson, A., Dolton, P., Reade, J. J., Schreyer, D., & Singleton, C. (2021). Causal effects of an absent crowd on performances and refereeing decisions during Covid-19. *Economics Letters, 198*, 109664.

Buraimo, B., Forrest, D., & Simmons, R. (2010). The 12th man?: Refereeing bias in English and German soccer. *Journal of the Royal Statistical Society: Series A (statistics in Society), 173*(2), 431–449.

Correia, M. (2019). *Una historia popular del fútbol*. Hoja de Lata editorial. Xixón, Asturies (España).

De Soto, A. Q. F. (2015). *Goles y banderas: fútbol e identidades nacionales en España*. Marcial Pons Historia.

Errekagorri, I., Castellano, J., Echeazarra, I., & Lago-Peñas, C. (2020). The effects of the video assistant referee system (VAR) on the playing time, technical-tactical and physical performance in elite soccer. *International Journal of Performance Analysis in Sport, 20*(5), 808–817.

Garicano, L., Palacios-Huerta, I., & Prendergast, C. (2005). Favoritism under social pressure. *Review of Economics and Statistics, 87*(2), 208–216.

Han, B., Chen, Q., Lago-Peñas, C., Wang, C., & Liu, T. (2020). The influence of the video assistant referee on the Chinese Super League. *International Journal of Sports Science & Coaching, 15*(5–6), 662–668.

Harvey, A. (2005). *Football: The first hundred years: The untold story*. Psychology Press.

Hesse, U. (2003). *Tor!: The story of German football*. WSC Books Limited.

Goldblatt, D. (2007). *The ball is round: a global history of football*. Penguin UK.

Kahneman, D., Knetsch, J. L., & Thaler, R. H. (1986). Fairness and the assumptions of economics. *Journal of business, 59*(S4), S285–S300.

Kahneman, D., Siboni, O., & Sunstein, C. (2021). *Noise: A flaw in human judgement*. Little Brown Spark.

Kolbinger, O. (2019). VAR experiments in the Bundesliga. In M. Armenteros, A. J. Benítez, & M. A. Betancor (Eds.), *The use of video technologies in refereeing football and other sports*. Taylor & Francis.

Konow, J. (2003). Which is the fairest one of all? A positive analysis of justice theories. *Journal of Economic Literature, 41*(4), 1188–1239.

Kranjec, A., Lehet, M., Bromberger, B., & Chatterjee, A. (2010). A sinister bias for calling fouls in soccer. *PloS One, 5*(7), e11667.

Kubayi, A., Larkin, P., & Toriola, A. (2021). The impact of video assistant referee (VAR) on match performance variables at men's FIFA World Cup tournaments. *Proceedings of the Institution of Mechanical Engineers, Part P: Journal of Sports Engineering and Technology*. https://doi.org/10.1177/175433712 1997581.

Lago-Peñas, C., Ezequiel, R., & Anton, K. (2019). How does video assistant referee (VAR) modify the game in elite soccer? *International Journal of Performance Analysis in Sport, 19*(4), 646–653.

Lago-Peñas, C., Gómez, M. A., & Pollard, R. (2020). The effect of the video assistant referee on referee's decisions in the Spanish LaLiga. *International Journal of Sports Science & Coaching*. https://doi.org/10.1177/174795412 0980111.

Moulin, H. (2004). *Fair division and collective welfare*. MIT press.

Reid, I., & Zisserman, A. (1996, April). Goal-directed video metrology. In *European conference on computer vision* (pp. 647–658). Springer.

Roemer, J. E. (1998). *Theories of distributive justice*. Harvard University Press.

Scanlon, T. M. (1977). Rights, goals, and fairness. *Erkenntnis, 11*(1), 81–95.

Scanlon, T. M. (1982). Contractualism and utilitarianism. In A. Sen & B. Williams (Eds.), *Utilitarianism and beyond*. Cambridge University Press.

Sen, A. K. (2009). *The idea of justice*. Harvard University Press.

Sen, A. (2017). Ethics and the foundation of global justice. *Ethics & International Affairs, 31*(3), 261–270.

Simón, J. A. (2019). VAR experiments in the Italian Serie A League. In M. Armenteros, A. J. Benítez, & M. A. Betancor (Eds.), *The use of video technologies in refereeing football and other sports*. Taylor & Francis.

Sperl, L., Hüttner, N., & Schroeger, A. (2021). Why do actions in slow motion appear to last longer? On the effect of video speed information. *Perception, 50*(1), 69–79.

Spitz, J., Moors, P., Wagemans, J., & Helsen, W. F. (2018). The impact of video speed on the decision-making process of sports officials. *Cognitive Research: Principles and Implications, 3*(1), 1–10.

Spitz, J., Wagemans, J., Memmert, D., Williams, A. M., & Helsen, W. F. (2021). Video assistant referees (VAR): The impact of technology on decision making in association football referees. *Journal of Sports Sciences, 39*(2), 147–153.

Taylor, R., & Jamrich, K. (2018). *Puskás sobre Puskás. Vida y gloria de una leyenda del fútbol*. Ed. Corner.

Tovar, J. (2014). *Números redondos*. Grijalbo.

Tovar, J. (2021). Soccer, World War II and coronavirus: A comparative analysis of how the sport shut down. *Soccer & Society, 22*(1–2), 66–74. https://doi.org/10.1080/14660970.2020.1755270

Waine, A., & Naglo, K. (Eds.). (2013). *On and off the field: Football culture in England and Germany*. Springer Publishing House.

Warren, C. (2019). VAR experiments in major league soccer (MLS). In M. Armenteros, A. J. Benítez, & M. A. Betancor (Eds.), *The use of video technologies in refereeing football and other sports*. Taylor & Francis.

Wernicke, L. (2017). *¿Por qué juegan once contra once?* Planeta Colombia.

Wilson, J. (2013). *Inverting the pyramid: The history of soccer tactics*. Bold Type Books.

INDEX